QUESTIONS AND
ANSWERS ON
COUNSELLING
IN *Action*

]8

COUNSELLING
· IN ACTION ·

Series editor: Windy Dryden

Counselling in Action is a series of books developed especially for counsellors and students of counselling which provides clear and explicit guidelines for counselling practice. A special feature of the series is the emphasis it places on the *process* of counselling.

Titles include:

Standards and Ethics for Counselling in Action
Tim Bond

Feminist Counselling in Action
Jocelyn Chaplin

Gestalt Counselling in Action
Petrūska Clarkson

Transcultural Counselling in Action
Patricia d'Ardenne and Aruna Mahtani

Hard-Earned Lessons from Counselling in Action
Edited by Windy Dryden

Key Issues for Counselling in Action
Edited by Windy Dryden

Psychodynamic Counselling in Action
Michael Jacobs

Person-Centred Counselling in Action
Dave Mearns and Brian Thorne

Transactional Analysis Counselling in Action
Ian Stewart

Cognitive-Behavioural Counselling in Action
Peter Trower, Andrew Casey and Windy Dryden

Psychosynthesis Counselling in Action
Diana Whitmore

QUESTIONS AND ANSWERS ON COUNSELLING

IN *Action*

EDITED BY
WINDY DRYDEN

SAGE Publications
London • Newbury Park • New Delhi

Introduction and editorial arrangement
© Windy Dryden 1993
Chapters 1, 7 and 29 © Dave Mearns 1993
Chapters 2 and 6 © Michael Jacobs 1993
Chapter 3 © Julia Segal 1993
Chapter 4 © Peter Ross 1993
Chapters 5a, 25 and 26 © Michael Barkham 1993
Chapter 5b © John Rowan 1993
Chapter 8 © Mark Aveline 1993
Chapter 9 © Jocelyn Chaplin 1993
Chapter 10 © Waseem J. Alladin 1993
Chapters 11 and 24a © Michael Carroll 1993
Chapter 12 © Vanja Orlans 1993
Chapter 13 © Elke Lambers 1993
Chapters 14 and 22 © Brian Thorne 1993
Chapter 15 © Moira Walker 1993
Chapter 16 © John C. Norcross and Thomas J. Tomcho 1993
Chapter 17 © Sue Wheeler 1993
Chapter 18 © Francesca Inskipp 1993
Chapter 19 © Jenifer Elton Wilson 1993
Chapters 20, 21 and 23 © Tim Bond 1993
Chapter 24b © Emmy van Deurzen-Smith 1993
Chapter 27 © Gladeana McMahon and Ken Powell 1993
Chapter 28 © David Pilgrim 1993
Chapter 30 © Colin Feltham 1993

First published 1993
Reprinted 1994

SAGE Publications Ltd
6 Bonhill Street
London EC2A 4PU

SAGE Publications Inc
2455 Teller Road
Newbury Park, California 91320

SAGE Publications India Pvt Ltd
32, M-Block Market
Greater Kailash – I
New Delhi 110 048

British Library Cataloguing in Publication Data

Questions and Answers on Counselling in Action. – (Counselling in Action Series)
  I. Dryden, Windy   II. Series
  616.89

  ISBN 0–8039–8858–3
  ISBN 0–8039–8859–1 Pbk

Library of Congress catalog card number 93–84341

Typeset by Mayhew Typesetting, Rhayader, Powys
Printed and bound in Great Britain by
Biddles Ltd, Guildford and King's Lynn

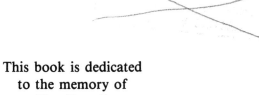

This book is dedicated
to the memory of
Ken Powell
who sadly died before
it was published

Contents

Part Three: The Personal and the Practical

Part Four: Beyond Specific Orientations

Part Five: Ethical Issues

Part Six: Professional Issues

Introduction

Whenever I have attended meetings or conferences on counselling, I have been impressed by the quality of questions asked by members of the audience. These questions reveal the concerns of both experienced and novice counsellors alike and often help to deepen thinking on topical issues in counselling.

Now that the *Counselling in Action* series has become well established as a useful resource for practitioners of counselling, I thought that the time was right to include in the series a volume devoted to answering questions from those working or studying in the field. Thus, for a period in 1991, I asked groups of experienced and trainee counsellors to submit anonymously and in writing questions that they would like answered by experts in the field. As you will see, some of the questions were addressed to named individuals who, without exception, agreed to provide written responses. Most questions, however, could be answered by a number of people and here I approached leading experts who again responded readily and enthusiastically. While the majority of questions were sent to one person for a response, on two occasions I sent the question to two people who I knew would provide contrasting viewpoints. I chose to do this because the issues concerned were particularly topical and differing opinions needed to be expressed.

My role in the process was as follows. First, I originated the idea for the book and secured the contract. Second, I elicited over fifty questions from experienced and trainee counsellors and selected the thirty questions that appear in the book. Third, I made minor grammatical and other changes to the wording of the questions before sending them to experts in the field to answer. Finally, I edited the respondents' first and subsequent drafts before handing the final manuscript to the publisher.

I wish to thank everybody who took part in this project: Sage – for backing my judgment; Susan Worsey – for her usual impeccable work; the anonymous questioners – for their provocative questions; and the respondents – for their thoughtful and full replies. I am sure you will agree that this book will provoke much lively discussion among experienced and trainee counsellors. As such it is a worthy addition to the series.

Windy Dryden

PART ONE

SPECIFIC ASPECTS OF PRACTICE

---

1 The core conditions

I have been a person-centred counsellor ever since I trained, several years ago. However, I have been becoming increasingly doubtful that the core conditions are necessary for therapeutic change, let alone sufficient. In your heart of hearts, have you ever harboured such doubts? If so, how did you resolve them, if indeed you have?

Dave Mearns

An adequate treatment of this question would require a sizeable chapter rather than the short space available here. In responding, then, I shall assume that the reader is familiar with the terms involved, or will be able to consult the referenced texts for definitions of terms such as 'constructive personality change' and the like. Even with this saving of space, my response has to be selective and therefore will not provide anything like a full analysis of the issues pertaining to the question of the necessity and sufficiency of the core conditions.

The hypotheses relating to the necessity and sufficiency of the core conditions were first published in the *Journal of Consulting Psychology* (Rogers, 1957). A more accessible reprint is available in *The Carl Rogers Reader* (Kirschenbaum and Henderson, 1990). Although this is the main research paper on the hypotheses, numerous other earlier works exist on the same subject, including a lecture entitled 'Some hypotheses regarding the facilitation of personal growth' delivered by Carl Rogers in 1954 and published in a later book (Rogers, 1961).

Most of the difficulty which practitioners have with the 'necessary and sufficient' hypotheses stems from a failure to realize that these are *research hypotheses*. It is self-evident that we could think of individual exceptions where one of the core conditions was not necessary and all taken together were insufficient. Proof of a hypothesis in the social science domain does not demand that it applies in every single case, but that it is positively linked to outcome to a statistically significant extent.

Rogers predicted that for constructive personality change to occur, it was necessary for the following conditions to exist and continue over a period of time:

1   two persons are in psychological contact;
2   the first, whom we shall call the client, is in a state of incongruence, being vulnerable or anxious;
3   the second person, whom we shall call the therapist, is congruent or integrated in the relationship;
4   the therapist experiences unconditional positive regard for the client;
5   the therapist experiences an empathic understanding of the client's internal frame of reference and endeavours to communicate this experience to the client;
6   the communication to the client of the therapist's empathic understanding and unconditional positive regard is to a minimal degree achieved (Kirschenbaum and Henderson, 1990: 221; Rogers, 1957: 96).

In presenting these hypotheses Rogers sought to stimulate the development of theory and research within psychotherapy and to bring into question many of the unvalidated assumptions existing in psychotherapeutic practice up to that time, in particular, assumptions around the necessity of processes such as assessment, diagnosis and diagnosis-related treatment. The hypotheses also implicitly denied the essential value to therapy of such techniques as interpretation of personality dynamics, free association, analysis of transference, hypnosis, suggestion or analysis of dreams. Techniques such as these would only be effective insofar as they provided channels for the basic core conditions. For example, while psychodynamic theory would regard *empathy* as a *channel for interpretation*, Rogers' basic hypotheses would turn this around and suggest that interpretation might be useful, not particularly for its content, but because it communicated the counsellor's empathy and regard.

Although it would be methodologically naive to assume that a research hypothesis should apply in every individual case, it is still interesting to consider the nature of exceptions. Presumably it is this exercise which was of interest to the person who framed the question, so I shall explore it further.

I do not have any particular difficulty with the *sufficiency* hypothesis. Where these six conditions exist it is difficult to imagine many cases where 'constructive personality change' would not follow. We might conjecture a gross act of manipulation by a personality disturbed client who for some reason wished to simulate a therapeutic process without actually engaging in it psychologically. It is certainly the case that the pathology of a minority of clients includes a need to *appear* to engage in the therapeutic process but in fact to bring it to a failed conclusion. However, even in this extreme scenario, the congruent and empathic counsellor would seek to work with that self-defeating syndrome.

I have in recent years pondered on whether these conditions are sufficient in the case of chronically disturbed clients. In particular I have wondered whether another condition must be framed around the size or sufficiency of the therapeutic context provided for the client. It seems clear to me that the size of the therapeutic context must at least be larger than the prison which the client has built around his or her self. In other words, the therapeutic environment which the helping institution is prepared to offer must be sufficiently encompassing for the client to accept the possibility of change and allow the glimmerings of hope to begin to counteract the fear which keeps them prisoner. I believe that there is much research to be done on the question of this *sufficiency of the therapeutic context*. However, whether this requires an extra hypothesis on top of the six framed by Rogers is questionable. It might be argued that establishing the sufficiency of the therapeutic context is a *pre-condition* which, in Rogers' formulation, would be encompassed within his underlying assumptions. An interesting glimpse of these is given in a later publication (Rogers, 1961: 344) where he made three assumptions to preface the basic hypotheses:

(a) a minimal willingness on the part of the two people to be in contact;
(b) an ability and minimal willingness on the part of each to receive communication from the other;
(c) assuming the contact to continue over a period of time.

In the light of these assumptions about 'willingness', the sufficiency of the therapeutic context might best be regarded as a *pre-counselling* variable, but it is nonetheless an important area for investigation.

While I see few individual exceptions to the notion of Rogers' conditions being *sufficient*, it is obvious that there are numerous instances where these conditions are not *necessary* for constructive personality change to occur. For example, many clients will exhibit constructive personality change even if the counsellor does absolutely nothing! Clients come into counselling at a time in their life when things are particularly bad. In such a circumstance there is statistically a much greater likelihood of the person moving in the direction of improvement rather than deterioration. This might be described in technical language as *statistical regression towards the mean* or, in idiomatic terms, as *the only way to go is up*. Even if the counsellor attempted to do precisely nothing with his clients, more would show improvement than deterioration over a period of time. Hence, if we were trying to apply Rogers' conditions to individual cases, we would find numerous examples where these conditions were not necessary.

Applying the idea of the necessity of these therapeutic conditions to individual clients with whom we might work is a decidedly un-person-centred procedure: before we have even met the client we are presuming what he or she needs! It is better to use the wisdom provided by theory and research as a general guide to our thinking rather than as offering us specific predictions on the individual client. Apart from anything else, this rigid way of thinking would make it impossible for us to understand the enormous diversity of the human individual and his or her sophistication with respect to self-protection and self-development. An outstanding example of this sophistication, and an individual exception to the hypothesis regarding the necessity of the therapeutic conditions, is described in the chapter written by Laura Allen in an earlier book in this series (Mearns and Dryden, 1990). In this chapter Allen describes her experience, as a client, of failure in counselling. Her counsellor was a man who appeared to offer none of the therapeutic conditions, indeed Laura Allen experienced him as emotionally abusive. Yet, it is also clear that the result of this abusive experience was to convert Laura's depression into anger and in that way it was to increase her personal power considerably.

In conclusion, I would want to assure the questioner that I do not have difficulty with the question of the necessity and sufficiency of the therapeutic core conditions: indeed I relish the vast amount of knowledge and understanding which these hypotheses have spawned.

References

Kirschenbaum, H. and Henderson, V. (eds) (1990) *The Carl Rogers Reader*. London: Constable.

Mearns, D. and Dryden, W. (eds) (1990) *Experiences of Counselling in Action*. London: Sage.

Rogers, Carl (1957) 'The necessary and sufficient conditions of psychotherapeutic personality change', *Journal of Consulting Psychology*, 21: 95–103.

Rogers, Carl (1961) *On Becoming a Person*. London: Constable.

2 The use of audio-tapes in counselling

I tape-record my counselling sessions, with my clients' permission of course, and find this a most valuable aid to self-supervision. I also play portions of tapes to my supervisor and learn much from her comments on what she hears. I should add that my supervision also involves more traditional case discussion methods. The two approaches complement each other very well. I understand that you have strong reservations about the use of audio-recordings of counselling sessions. Can you outline your objections and suggest why I should abandon this practice?

Michael Jacobs

My reservations about using tape-recordings have lessened somewhat since I first wrote about this (Jacobs, 1981). I was at that time particularly concerned through working as a supervisor with a counsellor who could not remember anything about clients except by taping. I was concerned for clients, and I did not permit the use of recording in the service of which I was then the head. My own approach is now less rigid; and I note that the questioner (and the supervisor) clearly use different methods and value the variety. There is increasing evidence from psychoanalytic practice, which held out for so long against the detailed recording of sessions, that there is now concern to encourage audio-recordings for research and training purposes (Aveline, 1991; Kachele et al., 1992). I myself now require students on some of the courses I teach to produce taped sessions; I have recently used tapes myself in research projects; and, as I describe later, I have even been asked by a client (and I agreed) to allow our sessions to be recorded by him.

I continue to have reservations about what the effect is on clients when they are asked to give permission (as they obviously must be asked), especially upon those who are compliant in helping the counsellor who 'needs it for my training', but who secretly feel cautious about being recorded. I hope that counsellors and supervisors who listen to tapes also listen out for indications that the client is anxious about the presence of the 'third ear' – the supervisor listening in at one remove. A psychodynamic approach cannot discount the relevance of anything that happens between counsellor and client, which includes the presence of a machine. Put another way, the observer inevitably influences the observations, with a tape-recorder doing precisely the same. Aveline writes, 'Being taped is never a neutral event' (1991: 352).

A rather fine illustration which confirms my concern about the client comes from someone else's client who happened to be talking to me about his sessions with his therapist that were taped week by week. The therapist used C90 tapes, where one side only lasted for the first 45 minutes of the session. This client held back some of his material until he heard the tape recorder switch itself off, because he did not want it to be heard on tape. While there appeared to be an element of triumph over the therapist in his account, there were clearly anxieties too. Perhaps the therapist realized what was happening, and listened particularly hard to the last 5 minutes of the session. If by some chance the supervisor also asked about what happened after the end of the tape, we can be relieved that the client's strategy was to no avail. I just wonder whether the therapist and the supervisor had any inkling of this, and if they did, what they made of it. Aveline is clearly aware of the issues (1991: 353). What is important from this example is not the actual tape-recording but the tape itself, and the games being played out through it – none of which, of course, could have been heard on tape.

The example illustrates a distinction I need to make, to clarify the reservations I still have, between the value of tape-recording for the training and technical development of the counsellor, and its value in understanding the client. I am aware in making this distinction that anything which improves the counsellor's skills and which broadens or deepens her expertise in counselling can extend the possibilities of understanding the client; and also that the content of the tape (even if, as in the case above, it is incomplete) will often help supervisor and counsellor extend their insight into what they hear. Nevertheless, there are other ways of achieving insight for which a tape-recording is unnecessary, and indeed may be a positive hindrance. An analogy which illustrates the point I want to make could be the obsessional client who tears up the paper from which he is reading his long list of symptoms, and closes the diary from which he is giving a blow-by-blow account of the week since the last session, and says, 'Let's forget all that. Let's talk about the real you and the real me.' It may not happen like that with the obsessional client, but perhaps it can (and I am sure it does) with a counsellor in supervision.

What I mean is that I can see the value of detail: that in training it can be of considerable advantage for a supervisor to hear a counsellor's tapes, since they are the most accurate record of the actual words spoken by the counsellor and the client, and of the speed and timing of interventions, including pauses and times of silence. I recognize too that when counsellors are being assessed, and where the award of qualifications depends upon accurate assessment, the submission of taped sessions (usually with an annotated transcript or a process report) acts as a check on whether counsellors do what they say and say what they do. I can also understand (although I would rarely want to do it myself) how playing parts of tapes in supervision, even when a counsellor is an experienced practitioner, can be valuable in picking up forgotten details, as well as in refining the more technical aspects of counselling, such as the way interventions are expressed, and how relevant they are to the actual words used by the client.

The moment when the obsessional throws away his list is significant. Listening in one supervision session to a counsellor describing in detail, from perfect notes, the sentence-by-sentence content of her session, I wanted to say: 'Stop. Can you put away the notes, and get on to the important bits?' Like her client, I felt she was holding back through the clutter of detail, and sure enough (because I did not like to interrupt), just at the end, too late for us to work on, the client too came to the point!

The psychodynamic approach, which for me is the richest of all the ways of understanding what a client is trying to express, accepts as axiomatic that communication between a counsellor and a client takes place on a number of different but simultaneous levels. There is one level (we might call it the conscious level, although that is too narrow a description) about which counsellors can learn from listening accurately to the actual words which the client and the counsellor use. It is not possible, for example, to hear a slip of the tongue without hearing it syllable by syllable. If this level concentrates upon the obvious, it can, like a slip of the tongue, point to the less obvious.

There is another level about which counsellors also need to learn, which for simplicity I will call unconscious communication, although this is again too narrow a description. It takes place, for example, in the counsellor's mind where it cannot be heard on tape – although I accept that playing the tape may trigger the same thoughts in supervision. This type of communication comes via words, but also despite words. It does not take place to order; it cannot be switched on with the tape. It may or may not occur in the counselling session, and it may or may not occur in supervision.

It may occur at other unlikely times, perhaps when I am driving my car, and see a hoarding, where an advertisement triggers off a thought about a client which I notice and absorb, but may even forget by the time I see the client next. It hopefully is allowed to happen in supervision, when I close my file of notes, when I turn off the tape, or when I hear my supervisory colleague's presentation. At such a time I may remember something completely different, that may even come from another session altogether, but which is yet another piece of evidence (or what the psychodynamic technique calls an association), another piece in the infinite and never-completed jigsaw, and another perspective on my client and on me. None of this comes about because I have taped a session, and indeed much of it comes about at the point when I become less concerned about accuracy, and word-for-word detail; when I cease to be interested in improving my technique; and even when I stop trying so hard to understand the client. That is why I believe that tapes may help technique, but be much less effective in helping us understand the client.

I might add that a client once asked to tape-record sessions with me. The reasons were many, although the ostensible one was to reflect upon the session afterwards (Dryden, 1981). I had the feeling that it was also to ensure that there was evidence if I said anything which was abusive, and that it was partly to put me on my mettle – which it did! In fact the tape proved unexpectedly useful, because from time to time I found myself saying: 'I think when you listen to the tape afterwards you will find I didn't say that but I did say this.' Sometimes I was right, once or twice I was wrong. What stands out, however, is not the accuracy of my memory, or the value of checking it against the tape, but that recording had a special significance for us both, that was much more than the chance for the client to listen to the actual words again.

Hence my reservations. All is not what it seems: and that is something I did not learn from a tape.

References

Aveline, M. (1991) 'The use of audio and videotape recordings of therapy sessions in the supervision and practice of dynamic psychotherapy', *British Journal of Psychotherapy*, 8: 347–58.

Dryden, W. (1981) 'Some uses of audio-tape procedures in counselling: a personal view', *Counselling*, 36: 14–17.

Jacobs, M. (1981) 'Setting the record straight', *Counselling*, 36: 10–13.

Kachele, H., Thoma, H., Ruberg, T. and Grunzig, H.-J. (1992) 'Audio-recordings of the psychoanalytic dialogue: scientific, clinical and ethical problems', in H. Dahl, H. Kachele and H. Thoma (eds), *Psychoanalytic Process Research Strategies*. Heidelberg: Springer Verlag.

3 Against self-disclosure

I understand that you are against the use of counsellor self-disclosure. I have found that disclosing some aspects of my life experience has had a profound therapeutic impact on several of my clients. Can you explain your objections to counsellor self-disclosure?

Julia Segal

I have several objections to counsellor self-disclosure. Some are a result of my training: some are based on my own experience when I have disclosed information about myself to clients and had cause later deeply to regret it.

It seems to me that there are several different types of self-disclosure and I am not sure which one you mean. Self-disclosure can range from 'I have two children' or 'I have the same illness as you do'; to 'I was in a similar situation and what I did was . . .' or 'You think I have nothing wrong in my life, well, in fact . . .'. In my view there are serious problems with any of these: though they are far more serious with the latter kind.

The first and most obvious objection is that the time in a counselling session is the client's: any time which is taken by a focus on the counsellor and their problems ('solved' or 'unsolved') is taken away from the client. Clients will not necessarily react to this at the time: many people have been brought up to assume that their claim on others' time is secondary, and to appear compliant when someone else takes from them something which is theirs. Some clients have been drawn into an inappropriate 'confidante' role by one or both parents and may attempt to repeat this with a counsellor rather than recognize the negative effects on them at the time as well as in the present.

I have heard several clients complain about a previous counsellor that 'She just wanted to talk about herself and her problems.' Once started it can be difficult to stop: if the client is given some information more questions may follow and the counsellor may then be faced with either a barrage of questions, totally distracting both from the work in hand, or the unpleasant necessity of saying 'No' and having to justify *this* refusal in the context of previous acquiescence. The difficulty of saying 'No' is simply put off when it could have been more productively and easily dealt with when it first arose. Similarly, the risks of disclosing to one client and not to another, when they may meet and compare notes, are obvious.

Talking about the counsellor is a means both client and counsellor can use to avoid serious and painful issues. When I was younger I found that a way of impressing people interviewing me for a job was to ask about them: this kind of flattery can make the interviewer feel good while preventing them from doing their task properly. I ended up feeling slightly contemptuous towards the interviewers for falling for it. A similar strategy may be used in counselling. The client knows on some level that their interest in the counsellor's life is a distraction: if the counsellor goes along with this it may reduce the client's belief in the counsellor's ability to work and to focus on and help the client.

The impact on the client of a disclosure cannot be predicted in advance. The counsellor may have one intention in telling the client something about themselves which the client understands in a completely different way. 'I've been in therapy too so I know how it feels' may not be reassuring but a sign that the counsellor is too mad to help. Knowing the sexual orientation of the counsellor or the number of children they have may mean to the client that their deepest conflicts about their own orientation or their own parental status cannot be openly acknowledged. If the client does not know about the counsellor the implications of the different possibilities may be explored, thus illuminating some of the client's own significant beliefs or attitudes.

There is also a problem to do with the counsellor's own motives for disclosing information. Many feelings, such as being challenged as useless or unfairly misjudged, can be aroused in a counsellor by some kind of direct question or assumption about their lives. An experienced and well-supported counsellor should be able to hold such feelings and to take them as some form of communication between the client and themselves, just as they would work with any other feelings which seem to have been evoked by the client. Simply answering the question may prevent the counsellor from really grasping and understanding the feelings conveyed.

A common point when self-disclosure can be tempting is when the client idealizes the counsellor; implying or actually saying that the counsellor is successful while they are a failure, for example. Melanie Klein, the psychoanalyst, was both clear and scathing about this when analysts were arguing in favour of self-disclosure as a means of combating idealization. She said that if the analyst paid more attention to the negative transference hidden behind the idealization they would discover that the client was not idealizing them at all but unconsciously seriously denigrating them. Her belief that 'idealization is a defence against denigration rather than reality' is one I have found extremely powerful and useful. Whenever I feel a client is idealizing me I look for hidden negative feelings: as Klein says, uncovering these can be very deflating as well as extremely important for the work.

A much better way to deal with requests for information is to explore with the client what it is that they are asking. Do they assume that no-one can understand them without having been through similar experiences themselves? This has serious implications which need to be discussed in terms of the people in their own lives who have and have not understood them. Are they feeling a longing to get closer to the counsellor, not wanting to be left out? These feelings need to be taken up and faced. Are they making insulting assumptions about the counsellor? The counsellor needs to look at these, take them seriously and consider the implications for the clients' feelings about themselves and those around them. Sometimes a client may be asked to guess the answer to their question, and this can lead to important clarification of their feelings, expectations and beliefs about the counsellor and whoever they represent in the client's past and present.

I think there is a particular difficulty if the counsellor discloses anything which could be construed as a problem. Knowledge of the counsellor's problems can make the client protective and add to difficulties in allowing themselves to 'burden' the counsellor with their own problems. (This can happen with unavoidable disclosures, for example, if the counsellor has a bad cold, looks ill or is pregnant.) Disclosure of the counsellor's successes can stimulate envy and hopelessness about ever living up to such achievements and a desire to make the counsellor learn the experience of failing. This may be hidden behind an overt sense of hope: 'If you can do it, so can I', which implies that differences between client and counsellor are irrelevant when they may not be. Clients' confusion of themselves and the counsellor is not uncommon and can make it harder for the client to truly find their own voice, their own self. Disclosure of similarities between client and counsellor can add to this confusion, which may be the counsellor's as well as the client's. A counsellor identifying with a client has a serious problem which should be dealt with in supervision and/or the counsellor's own therapy.

Working in the disability field I have heard many arguments about the value of people counselling others with the same illness or disability. I think it is helpful to distinguish between different kinds of help offered in different contexts. There is an important place for successful role models outside the counselling room. It can also be useful to have a telephone help-line staffed entirely by people who have a particular condition and 'know about it from the inside'. However, even here there may be some kind of illusion involved. Nobody's illness is just the same as anyone else's any more than any person's divorce or marriage is the same as another's. Conversely, someone with a particular health condition who has been well trained as a counsellor may be very well placed to counsel someone else with another condition entirely, and also to counsel people who are perfectly healthy. The issues of so-called 'peer counselling' in my experience sometimes cover a deep sense that an ill or disabled counsellor is 'unfit' to counsel anyone other than an 'unfit' client. Here the disclosure of a health condition may be a way of warding off feelings about the differences between people with and without certain health problems rather than openly working with these differences and the feelings and difficulties they bring.

Clearly self-disclosure depends on the situation as well as on the counsellor. Some counsellors do disclose their own health status; some cannot help disclosure of, for example, the fact that they use a wheelchair; some find it better to avoid self-disclosure as much as possible and to use conscious or unconscious questions about the counsellor's state of health as they would any other material. Where a question carries an implication of 'second-class status' for example, it may be very useful to examine the client's feelings about not knowing whether the counsellor has the same status as they do. Clients' feelings about the significance of their own health may be clarified and challenged more easily in this examination of their attitudes to the counsellor.

Refusing to answer questions about the self has to be handled carefully, otherwise clients can be silently hurt and upset at the 'rudeness' involved. I think that the first time it arises the client should be given a brief explanation on the lines of 'I don't answer questions about myself: it seems to be more useful to look at what you are asking rather than simply to answer directly.' The client's feelings about this, their possible hurt, anger, a sense of having said something wrong or of being put down have to be sensed and acknowledged immediately and sympathetically. The issue of who is in control of the session, and whether it is going to be run the way the counsellor thinks is best may need to be brought into the open. Being 'client-centred' does not mean doing everything the client wants you to do. It may be helpful sometimes to make a direct contrast between a counselling relationship and a social one.

A refusal to enter into a social relationship, or to answer enquiries about oneself may give permission to the client to be self-centred and make it clear that counselling is for the client and that they do not have to worry about asking the polite questions and being normally considerate about the counsellor's feelings. The advantages and disadvantages of the differences between a social and professional relationship should be clearly understood by the counsellor and aspects of this may need at times to be picked up with a client.

Finally, there are issues of power, control and privacy involved. Knowledge does give a kind of power. Counsellors expose many aspects of their working self to clients: they may be deeply involved emotionally during the session. By making clear boundaries between what is available to clients and what is not, the counsellor's own sense of security is enhanced and the freedom to be emotionally involved, even with clients who are in some way unpleasant or threatening, is increased. If a client knows too much about a counsellor the counsellor may at times find themselves unconsciously withdrawing emotionally in order to protect their privacy.

Summary

There are many reasons for counsellors not to disclose information about themselves. Discussion of the counsellor's experience takes the focus off the client. It can be a means of avoiding serious and painful issues, both for the client and for the counsellor. In particular it can prevent confrontation of issues about the client's belief in the counsellor's competence and the difficulties of two people being different from each other. There is really no predicting what any disclosure will mean to a client, and it may simply confuse the issues and increase the client's protectiveness towards the counsellor. It also removes the possibility of uncovering and examining the client's assumptions about the counsellor, some of which may be false but very illuminating. Lastly, I maintain, it is important for the counsellor to retain privacy and clear boundaries in the relationship in order to be free to use their empathy to the full in the service of the client.

Editor's note

Interested readers might like to consult *Self-Disclosure in Therapeutic Relationships*, edited by G. Stricker and M. Fisher (Plenum Press, New York, 1990) for differing views on counsellor self-disclosure.

4 Using hypnosis in counselling

When, for what purpose and how can hypnosis be introduced in counselling?

Peter Ross

The when and how issues are very intertwined and will be dealt with first. The possibility of using hypnosis does not excuse a counsellor the normal process of assessment: of the client problem, of the resources a client brings to counselling, of client ideas and preferences regarding their wishes for help, of making a judgment and contract with regard to boundaries and procedures.

When hypnosis is suggested by the client

Some clients will approach a counsellor saying 'I want hypnosis.' Often accompanying this is the fantasy that they will go into a sleep like insensible state where all volition is lost, and all responsibility forgone. Often present also is the idea that they will be totally controlled by the counsellor and that when they wake up the problem will be gone. Part of the assessment must be an exploration of such hidden agendas and great care exercised in such cases.

When hypnosis is suggested by the counsellor

Should no mention of hypnosis be made by the client, a counsellor might best introduce the subject casually: 'Well, I suppose hypnosis is one of those things we might consider along with . . .'. The client response will reveal much of their assumptive framework about the nature of hypnosis and indicate whether it is worth pursuing the subject at all, or doing some pre-induction education. As with any normal population, some clients will be very receptive hypnotic subjects, some very unreceptive and most in the middle. Training can make a considerable difference (Robertson, 1992). Several sessions spent helping a client enhance responsiveness may sometimes be worthwhile. The rapport built during the process of assessment, education and skills training is critically important to successful induction. It is of lesser importance only with a very small group of highly susceptible clients. Those learning to induce hypnosis fail most frequently because of a desire to 'get on' with hypnosis rather than pay due time and attention to such foundations.

It is possible to use hypnotic susceptibility scales (Fellows, 1988) to select appropriate clients. However, the time required can as easily be spent trying out a few basic induction procedures (Edmonston, 1986) which as often as not will give the information required. This also will give the client skills and relaxed confidence, as well as so frequently actually producing a light hypnosis that, with only a pause to ensure client contentment and assent, one can just get on with deepening the hypnosis and using the chosen therapeutic procedures.

Selecting 'chosen therapeutic procedures' is a function of the counsellor's grasp of human dynamics, clinical training and experience. Hypnosis is an adjunct to therapy, not a therapy in itself. Putting somebody 'into' hypnosis and 'out' again has no more therapeutic effect than does an anaesthetic without surgery. Counsellors should ensure they have completed a recognized training programme[1] as well as have appropriate supervision to hand before working with clients. There is considerable disagreement among both researchers and practitioners about the fundamental nature of hypnosis. Thus, when a client quite innocently but reasonably asks 'What is hypnosis?' one is faced with a dilemma. Does one give a 2-hour lecture in an effort to convey one's personal conviction about the 'true facts?' Does one give a dispassionate analysis of the research and end up with lots of confusing questions rather than clear answers? Or does one try to be pragmatic and recognize what is behind the question? The client usually wants reassurance as well as information. Any ideas which will help the client predict and cope with what will happen if hypnosis is used will be reassuring.

Metaphors and inductions

Descriptions of hypnosis are not so much 'true' as metaphorical. The nature of the metaphor matters a lot in hypnosis. It not only describes, it prepares. It filters and structures attention. So even if the client does *not* ask about the nature of hypnosis, the counsellor will often deliberately raise the question. Thus to an engineer client we might describe hypnosis in terms of signal detection theory. To a film critic client we might talk about the way a film director sets up cues to seduce us. As metaphors they are neither true nor false descriptions of hypnosis or hypnotic procedures, just pragmatic ways of helpfully conveying reality for a specific person in a specific context. 'Good' metaphors, which we can now understand as person-tailored ones, greatly facilitate compliance with the therapist's instructions, and the 'depth' of hypnosis reached by the client.

Selecting metaphors for describing the nature of hypnosis, which by implication begin to describe for the client what induction or series of inductions may be about to be used with the client, constitutes an important part of any training programme. In the education and clinical setting in which most counsellors work, and with the core ethics of counselling in mind, metaphors which emphasize a client taking responsibility for his or her own active involvement in the induction are not only likely to be most acceptable but are often most effective too.

Thus for our film critic client one could describe hypnosis as being like going to the cinema. One might say:

> We stare at a bright screen in the darkness, and while physically relaxed (Edmonston, 1981) we become mentally alert and focus upon the cues the director has provided to draw us into the action. Gradually we become more and more involved, even at the point of crying when the hero dies. By analogy when deeply immersed in reading a good novel we may not be aware of somebody calling us. Yet, when they call a second time, are suddenly aware the call is the second call. We are, to some extent, 'locked in' in such situations, by filtering information both in and out. In a natural setting we can all have filtering out experiences. Dragged half unwillingly to the cinema by a friend, we can 'distance' ourselves and prevent involvement by thinking of the huge fees paid to the actors, focus on the technical tricks and not the story line, and so on.

Encouraging clients to become actively involved in immersing themselves in the story line using all the film director's skills and others (Robertson, 1992) greatly improves speed of induction and 'depth' of hypnosis. The skills are frequently simple: 'Do not just walk across the grass in your imagination, smell the new-mown grass as you walk.'

It is very inconvenient to have to spend lots of time each session repeating such 'chats', which are really informal pre-induction procedures, so that once a client has achieved any depth of hypnosis at all the counsellor needs to take advantage of more rapid induction possibilities. The main one is post-hypnotic suggestion. When in hypnosis, clients are given the suggestion that when they return to a specific situation in a specific way, a simple formula (say, counting from 1 to 10) will re-trigger the hypnotic depth quite automatically, and without all the time-wasting preliminaries. One can separate induction and therapy or, with skill and experience, begin to merge one into the other from the outset (Gilligan, 1987), even from the beginning of assessment just in case hypnosis may be an option to be employed later. This can save considerable time.

Complications of strategy and structure

So far, we have assumed that the subject of hypnosis is introduced by the client as the opening move, or that the counsellor makes the suggestion following assessment. But what about introducing hypnosis mid-way through a series of sessions? The therapeutic stances favoured by individual counsellors may be divided into those in which the counsellor takes primary responsibility for process, and those in which primary responsibility is taken for outcome. The recently developed very short-term psychodynamic therapies, and also cognitive/behavioural therapies, tend to be of the latter kind. Long-term psychoanalysis serves as an example of the former.

When working long term, one has the 'luxury' of focusing at length on processes, such as, say, parallels between the relationship of client to parent and client to counsellor. The fact that the presenting problem *was* a problem, will be deliberately and temporarily forgotten. It is assumed that 'the problem' will come right without being directly addressed, if the underlying dynamics are reformed. In taking primary responsibility for outcome, no such assumption is made; the 'symptom' being addressed more directly. Therapeutic systems have to stand at some point on the spectrum between these poles.

Where the counsellor is working in such a way as to take primary responsibility for process, the introduction of hypnosis during counselling should be avoided by all but the most experienced. The reason for this is simple. If for many sessions the counsellor has largely confined him or her self to working with process, with responsibility for other initiatives with the client, the introduction of hypnosis reverses the situation. A shift in the burden of the type of responsibility accepted by each party can of course be negotiated and re-negotiated. But it is so fundamental to the dynamics of the relationship that, once the original pattern has been broken, it is exceptionally difficult to get back to it. Inherent in this difficulty is the fact that, by taking this different level of responsibility, the counsellor has revealed him or herself in such a way that any transference phenomena, whether latent or realized, are made far more complex than before. Reverting to the original pattern, or attempting to do so, results in novel transference phenomena which few are trained to deal with. These complexities are best avoided by not using hypnosis in such situations. It can seldom be essential to do so.

No such difficulties are encountered where the counsellor has already been taking primary responsibility for outcome. Should one wish to introduce hypnosis as another tool from the toolbag, one simply waits for an appropriate natural break in the transition from one phase of work to another. There is subsequently no problem in re-establishing the original pattern of relationship.

Indications for hypnosis

For what purpose might one wish to use hypnosis in counselling? Many hypnotic inductions use relaxation procedures, and self-hypnosis may be used to reach deep levels of relaxation. Self-hypnosis is a favourite procedure for those suffering from bronchial asthma, for example. Counsellors frequently encounter psychosomatic symptoms such as irritable bowel syndrome, hyperventilation, peptic ulcer, ulcerative colitis or skin disorders. Hypnosis has a very good outcome record in these fields.[2] Effective counselling requires client attention to be available. Panic attacks, pain and other attention-distracting factors can readily be controlled with short-term hypnosis, so allowing conventional counselling a chance to get under way. Many behaviourial problems such as smoking and eating pattern disorders may be helped with hypnosis, though often most effectively in combination with non-hypnotic approaches.

Hypnosis may also be used, as in age regression, to help the client to feel as if they are really returning to a previous age and situation and thereby exploring it, for repressed or forgotten material. It should be emphasized that the client controls this, not the counsellor. It should also be emphasized that the uncovering and recovery of such materials is distinct from its use in counselling. Considerable effort in conventional counselling must still be made to help the client integrate the material, explore the meaning of it and deal with any process implications which it may have.

Contra-indications for hypnosis

As indicated earlier, caution needs to be exercised with clients who *insist* on hypnosis. More explicit contra-indications would be the psychoses, ideas with paranoid overtones and attributions of influence to ghosts, etc. Suicidal ideation is also a contra-indication, though not depression itself. It may readily be seen that hypnosis is a powerful tool. As such it calls for more training, more competence and more confidence in one's basic professional training as a counsellor, rather than less. Hypnosis is an adjunct to this professional training, not a substitute for it.

Notes

1   Enquiries regarding courses and membership of the British Society for Experimental and Clinical Hypnosis may be made to Dr Michael Heap, Dept. of Psychology, Middlewood Hospital, Sheffield S6 1TP, UK.
2   For an overview of the range of problems to which hypnosis may be applied, together with assessments of outcome, see Crasilneck and Hall (1985). Also see the other chapters in Heap (1988).

References

Crasilneck, H.B. and Hall, J.A. (1985) *Clinical Hypnosis* (2nd edn). New York: Grune & Stratton.

Edmonston, W. (1981) *Hypnosis and Relaxation*. New York: Wiley.

Edmonston, W. (1986) *The Induction of Hypnosis*. New York: Wiley.

Fellows, B. (1988) 'The use of hypnotic susceptibility scales', in Michael Heap (ed.), *Hypnosis: Current Clinical, Experimental, and Forensic Practices*. London: Croom Helm.

Gilligan, S. (1987) *Therapeutic Trances*. New York: Brunner/Mazel.

Heap, M. (ed.) (1988) *Hypnosis: Current Clinical, Experimental, and Forensic Practices*. London: Croom Helm.

Robertson, L. (1992) 'Modifying hypnotic susceptibility with the Carleton Skills Training Program: a replication', *Contemporary Hypnosis*, 9 (2): 97–103.

5a Counselling for a brief period

What are the advantages and disadvantages of brief counselling?

Michael Barkham

There are a range of advantages and disadvantages of brief counselling. However, before considering each in turn, a few points of definition are worth noting.

Definitions

Brief counselling can be defined as comprising between one and twenty sessions with around six sessions often being reported as the average duration. Phillips (1991) reported data on a sample of 1.4 million cases in the US showing the median number of therapy sessions to be 3.8 sessions with the mean in the range of six to eight sessions. Brief counselling can occur 'naturally' (i.e. initially open-ended but both parties subsequently agreeing to terminate within twenty or so sessions) or be 'planned' (i.e. both parties agreeing a contract at the outset for a specific number of sessions). Planned counselling is more likely to occur within brief rather than longer-term counselling and the literature on planned interventions has been fully reviewed (for example, Bloom, 1992).

When considering the issue of counselling process, brief counselling clearly differs from longer-term counselling. Bloom (1992) presents five hallmarks of planned brief therapy/counselling: (1) prompt intervention, (2) higher level of therapist activity, (3) targeting specific but limited goals, (4) identifying a clear focus and (5) setting a time limit. For example, the *goals* are more limited. Bloom (1981: 183) views the central question being addressed in any form of brief intervention as follows: 'What have these clients failed to understand about their lives that could make a difference in how they are conducting themselves now and how they might manage their lives in the future?' Accordingly, brief counselling does not aim to achieve characterological change. The point to be made here, and throughout this answer, is that brief counselling is *different* from longer-term counselling. It is not simply providing less counselling: it has a different structure and a different process. However, research findings indicate brief counselling to be as effective as time-unlimited counselling: 'Virtually without exception . . . empirical studies of short-term out-patient psychotherapy . . . have found that planned short-term psychotherapies are essentially equally effective and are, in general, as effective as time-unlimited psychotherapy' (Bloom, 1992: 9). That being the case, there are arguments for and against the practice of brief counselling.

Advantages

In terms of advantages, five specific areas can be identified: (1) treatment of choice, (2) service provision, (3) community versus individual needs, (4) developmental life-span approach and (5) applications. Each of these will be addressed in turn.

Treatment of choice

First, whilst not explicitly an advantage specific to brief counselling, it is important to state that brief counselling is the treatment of choice for many presenting problems (Rawson, 1992). This is critical because it counters two falsehoods: first, that receiving more counselling is, by its very nature, a better option, and second, that clients who receive brief counselling are somehow being 'short changed'. For example, research findings suggest that clients presenting with low levels of depression benefit from eight sessions and show no further gains after receiving a further eight sessions (Shapiro and Barkham, 1992). By contrast, clients presenting with more severe levels of depression showed continued gains when administered a second series of eight sessions. While brief counselling is the treatment of choice in terms of outcome for many clients, it is also the treatment of choice at the level of the counselling process. The structure of brief counselling provides many clients with a framework which can instil more active work. This infrastructure assists the counsellor working in brief counselling towards a simple goal: 'the alleviation of people's "pain" in the shortest time possible' (Rawson, 1992: 107).

Service provision

Second, the development of brief models would appear to be more consistent with the realities of service provision. If the average duration of psychological interventions is reportedly about six sessions, then it would seem sensible to be developing and devising *planned* models of intervention which are consistent with this demand. In terms of the duration of counselling offered, the *resources* of the service delivery system are a critical consideration.

Howard (1988) estimated that in the US there are only sufficient resources to provide all referred clients within a one-year period with three sessions of therapy. No equivalent data exist on the issue of resource–needs matching within the UK. Clearly, this raises the question of *who* is to get the available services. At present, service providers are presented with the problem of deciding who, in terms of clientele, has priority needs over others to receive the limited resources available. In terms of the amount of counselling clients expect, considerable differences have been reported between therapists' and clients' preferences (Pekarik and Wierzbicki, 1986). Defining short-term therapy as one to fifteen sessions and long-term therapy as sixteen or more sessions, 65 per cent of therapists preferred long-term therapy as against only 20 per cent of clients who expected it.[1] The suggestion here is that it might be informative to determine the client's perspective.

Community versus individual needs
Third, although counselling addresses the needs of the individual, individuals comprise a given community and service providers need to be aware of the needs of the community. Counselling has to balance the tensions of meeting the needs of the person currently 'in counselling' versus the needs of the many individuals in the community whose needs are not being met by the service providers. When seeing an ongoing client for a further, for example, eight sessions, it is salutary to consider the alternative course of action of offering a new client those eight sessions. Findings from research show that a given number of counselling sessions does not lead to the same degree of improvement later in counselling as it would have had early in the treatment. While more counselling sessions result in a greater number of clients reporting improvement, there are diminishing returns as counselling continues. For example, Howard et al. (1986) found approximately one-third of clients to show 'measurable improvement' after three sessions, half after eight sessions, and three-quarters after twenty-six sessions. In order to balance briefer contracts of counselling, maintenance or 'booster' sessions could be scheduled which would provide clients with a framework for further work and help reduce the possibility of relapse.

Developmental life-span approach
Fourth, models of brief counselling are consistent with a life-span developmental approach in which people have differing needs at differing times in their lives (Bennett, 1984), some of which can be anticipated (e.g. children moving away from home or retirement)

while others may not (e.g. sudden breakdown in a significant relationship or being made redundant at short notice). This is similar to the notion of what has been termed a 'treatment episode' model, allowing issues to be addressed in an individual's life at many times. Accordingly, a treatment relationship may extend across time, interspersed by a number of brief treatment episodes. Shectman writes: 'Viewed in this way, brief therapy is more a function of the frame of mind of the therapist than the actual time span or the number of hours of treatment' (1986: 523).

Applications

And fifth, brief counselling models have considerable utility in the context of industry and organizations. For example, it is reported that stress-related illness costs the UK £7 billion a year in terms of lost production, sick pay and NHS charges (Buckingham, 1992). One response has been the emergence of Employee Assistance Programmes (EAPs). For example, Whitbread provide an EAP in which the first three sessions are paid for by the company. This limited contract necessitates counsellors having the ability to provide a service within those constraints. The availability of brief intervention models has clear efficacy within such settings (for example, Barkham and Shapiro, 1990; Taylor et al., 1992). Further applications come in the form of 'well-being' clinics in which individuals seek counselling in advance of their experiencing distress (for example, prior to major transitions in their lives, retirement, etc.).

Disadvantages

In terms of disadvantages, four areas are addressed: (1) misuses and misperceptions; (2) relapse and maintenance, (3) assignment and (4) process issues.

Misuses and misperceptions

First, all counselling models can be misused. In longer-term counselling, dependency needs can be abused and clients can be kept in counselling long after they need to be. In brief counselling, client defences can be opened and not satisfactorily resolved, making them feel abandoned when counselling is terminated long before it is prudent to do so. The most appropriate response to these situations is to ensure that careful assessment is carried out and clients' responses to counselling monitored through statutory follow-up. The collection of such data provides a check on the status of individual clients following counselling and also builds potential data sets which can inform and/or challenge previously held perceptions of models of counselling in the scientific community. Two implications arise. First, practitioners should be open-minded when assessing a client's needs: a client may require long-term counselling or equally may be better suited for some form of brief counselling. The client who is offered brief counselling may, as a result of subsequent work, be deemed to require further counselling. The second point is that practitioners should not work within models of counselling (that is, orientations as well as durations) in which they do not feel at ease. The skills required in one model are different from those required in another, and counselling as a discipline is the richer for pursuing a path of substantiating the effectiveness of the diverse models it has to offer through continued scientific enquiry.

Relapse and maintenance
Second, there is increasing concern about relapse rates and the failure to maintain gains from counselling. For example, with reference to clients meeting criteria for Major Depressive Disorder (MDD), Shea et al. reported that '16 weeks of . . . treatment[s] is insufficient treatment to achieve full recovery and lasting remission for most outpatients with MDD' (1992: 785). Although most clients showed improvement, only 24 per cent of those who entered treatment and had complete follow-up data both recovered *and remained well*. Accordingly, it may not just be the level of the presenting problem which may determine length of counselling, but also the level and robustness of the state of well-being sought as a result of counselling.

Assignment
Third, it is possible for clients to under-present their problems at initial interview or alternatively under-score on any intake or screening instrument. While initial presentation may suggest a brief counselling intervention is appropriate, this should always be seen as falsifiable, if evidence presents itself. For example, where clients present with very vague notions of what is troubling them, this may be a cue that longer duration counselling is required. Similarly, if clients are seeking a more reflective process, then the pacing afforded by longer-term counselling may be more appropriate. Concerns are often expressed about the suitability of clients for brief counselling. In response, there is general agreement on the contra-indications for brief counselling: clients who cannot attend to the counselling process, who have presenting problems better suited to other interventions, or clients who do not have

sufficient ego strength. Accordingly, any decision about the amount (i.e. duration) of counselling a client will receive should be a matter of as much consideration as the type (that is, theoretical orientation) of counselling they will receive (see Burlingame and Fuhriman, 1987).

Process issues

Fourth, process issues need to be clearly addressed and, in particular, termination issues recognized from the very beginning of the counselling contract. This process clearly alters the dynamic of the counselling situation and differentiates it from longer-term counselling. Counsellors need to consider carefully whether issues raised in brief counselling can be brought to a point of closure within the agreed time-frame. This requires different skills from longer-term counselling and has implications for training and supervision. A major component of the process of counselling is the client–counsellor relationship. It is clearly important for clients in brief counselling to experience the counsellor as responsive to their needs.

Conclusion

Whatever the differences between brief and longer-term counselling, the demands on both counsellor and client are high and it would be important for the practitioner not to confuse the term 'brief' counselling with 'easy' counselling. The most parsimonious view is that brief counselling is 'different', comprising some components of longer-term counselling but not others. Whilst different, brief counselling can demand the same potential for client work as longer-term counselling. In the end counsellors will undoubtedly have their own personal preferences as to how they work in counselling. However, even if they have a preference in practice for brief or for longer-term counselling, it would be hoped that their respective place in the discipline of counselling will be equally informed both by the findings from research studies and the views of clients themselves.

Note

1 The original paper miscalculates this figure as 12 per cent.

References

Barkham, M. and Shapiro, D.A. (1990) 'Brief psychotherapeutic interventions for job-related distress: a pilot study of Prescriptive and Exploratory therapy', *Counselling Psychology Quarterly*, 3: 133–47.

Bennett, M.J. (1984) 'Brief psychotherapy and adult development', *Psychotherapy*, 21: 171–7.

Bloom, B.L. (1981) 'Focussed single-session therapy: initial development and evaluation', in S.H. Budman (ed.), *Forms of Brief Therapy*. New York: Guilford Press.

Bloom, B.L. (1992) *Planned Short-Term Psychotherapy*. Boston: Allyn & Bacon.

Buckingham, L. (1992) 'A headache that just won't go', *The Guardian*, 31 October: 38.

Burlingame, G.M. and Fuhriman, A. (1987) 'Conceptualizing short-term treatment: a comparative review', *The Counseling Psychologist*, 15: 557–95.

Howard, K.I. (1988) 'The psychotherapeutic service delivery system', keynote address, International Meeting of the Society for Psychotherapy Research, Toronto.

Howard, K.I., Kopta, S.M., Krause, M.S. and Orlinsky, D.E. (1986) 'The dose-effect relationship in psychotherapy', *American Psychologist*, 41: 159–64.

Pekarik, G. and Wierzbicki, M. (1986) 'The relationship between clients' expected and actual treatment duration', *Psychotherapy*, 23: 532–4.

Phillips, E.L. (1991) 'George Washington University's international data on psychotherapy delivery systems: modeling new approaches to the study of therapy', in L.E. Beutler and M. Crago (eds), *Psychotherapy Research: An International Review of Programmatic Studies*. Washington, DC: American Psychological Association.

Rawson, P. (1992) 'Focal and short-term psychotherapy is a treatment of choice', *Counselling*, 3: 106–7.

Shapiro, D.A. and Barkham, M. (1992) 'Choosing the treatment that you can afford', Paper presented at the symposium on Psychotherapy in the marketplace: Responding to the NHS reforms. Annual meeting of the Association of University Teachers of Psychiatry, University of Warwick.

Shea, M.T., Elkin, I., Imber, S.D., Sotsky, S.M., Watkins, J.T., Collins, J.F., Pilkonis, P.A., Beckham, E., Glass, D.R., Dolan, R.T. and Parloff, M.B. (1992) 'Course of depressive symptoms over follow-up', *Archives of General Psychiatry*, 49: 782–7.

Shectman, F. (1986) 'Time and the practice of psychotherapy', *Psychotherapy*, 23: 521–5.

Taylor, E., Shapiro, D.A. and Folkard, S. (1992) 'Designing a therapeutic intervention for a specific population', Paper presented at the Third Annual Meeting of the Special Group in Counselling Psychology, Birmingham.

5b Counselling for a brief period

What are the advantages and disadvantages of brief counselling?

John Rowan

How brief is brief? Some people have written of brief counselling as being thirty sessions or so; Strupp (1978) suggests that twenty to forty sessions is optimal. Butcher and Koss (1978) say 'Today, most practitioners agree that 25 sessions is the upper limit' and also that many clinicians recommend from one to six sessions. Crisis counselling is often restricted to three to five sessions. The latest version I have seen is the two-plus-one formula of Barkham (1989), where he suggests two sessions a week apart and then another one three months later. Personally I would define as brief any counselling where there was a definite limited contract of any kind, and Ursano and Dressler (1974) support this view.

I have occasionally done that myself. I remember one case where a woman lived in Leeds, and only had the money to come to London three times. So we fixed up six meetings, on Monday afternoons and Tuesday mornings, so that she could stay just the one night in London each week for three weeks. Her problem was the limited one of social anxiety, so it seemed quite appropriate to try this, and it worked very well.

In general, I think something brief is always worth trying first, particularly if the problem is a specific one. I have seen some good accounts of very brief but successful treatments of fear of flying, exam nerves, stage fright and the like, some only lasting for one session.

What I feel very unhappy about, however, is the suggestion that brief counselling should take the place of more long-term counselling in most cases. For example, Garfield (1977) suggests that about two-thirds of clients will respond well to short-term counselling. Barkham suggests (Dryden and Barkham, 1990) that one-third is nearer the mark, so there is no real consensus on this. My reason for objecting is that it seems to me that people very often come into counselling at a very important stage in their lives, when they are ready to reconsider their existence and their whole way of life. At about the age of 33, give or take three years, a crisis hits them: they become redundant, or their partner leaves them, or they run into high stress levels one way or another. They go into counselling or psychotherapy (in this context the two seem to me to be interchangeable) due to the immediate unhappiness created by the crisis.

At this point counselling can flatter them by saying to them in effect that they are fine, and that the crisis will soon be over, and that they can then go back to being just the way they were before, as Butcher and Koss (1978) put it, 'prompt re-establishment of the client's previous emotional equilibrium'. This is the familiar promise of adjustment to the existing order, often finely disguised by using such phrases as 'the goals of counselling should be the client's, not the counsellor's'. It is achieved by contracts and programmes and conscious cognitive sorting out of the problems, and a 'firm refusal to broaden the objectives' as time goes on.

The question of phases

Alternatively, counselling can say to them in effect that they now have an opportunity to take a fresh look at themselves, and start on what could be a life-changing project. It can say to them that this is an initiation, a journey into the labyrinth, where they may meet and deal with some of the most fundamental issues that life can give and come out again transformed. Their personality, their character, can change.

In long-term counselling there are normally three phases, as Kopp (1977) has pointed out rather elegantly. In phase one, the initial symptoms are dealt with, and a reasonable degree of success is achieved in disposing of them. This has to do with the immediate alleviation of pain.

In phase two, deeper issues are tackled, which might not have been evident at all at the beginning, but which now seem to be important. For example, in the course of counselling, some clients discover that they were sexually abused as children, which they were not consciously aware of at all when they came into counselling. To leave the client at this point because the contract did not anticipate such an eventuality seems abusive to me. Similarly, but much more frequently, many clients discover that their childhood was not the idyllic or bland experience they had previously thought, but was in fact a hotbed of emotions and decision-making. During this phase the client may at times feel worse rather than better, and any crude attempt to measure improvement can go astray at this point. Research designs on the whole do not even attempt to do justice to this phase, perhaps sometimes being funded by organizations intent on saving money.

Third, there is the phase of working through the implications for daily life of the discoveries made during the counselling experience. This bridging activity, between new self-concepts and action in the everyday world, is often a lengthy process, where there may be setbacks and errors which need to be dealt with.

It seems to me that brief counselling ignores the second phase, and in effect cheats the client of the potential hidden within their crisis. It sticks to the easy part, the part where some immediate results can be seen, and ignores the more demanding parts, where there may be difficulties with the therapeutic relationship itself. It is in the second phase that higher levels of skill and deeper levels of self-knowledge are called for on the part of the counsellor.

What are the motives?

I have no quarrel with brief counselling as such, but I do have a worry about the way in which it is being pushed and peddled at times as the answer to everything. I also have a worry about data purporting to show that in practice counselling is pretty short – I have seen figures of five sessions or so being bandied about – because this covers up all the problems of averaging. Also this leads to the question being asked – 'If we can get away with such brief counselling, how brief can we make it?' This is the logic of 'service delivery' and other such concepts, based on a mechanistic cost–benefit analysis. The end-point of such considerations is the proposal that we should adopt the 'two-plus-one model' of counselling (Barkham, 1989), where the client is seen for only two sessions, with a follow-up session three months later. This seems to me like a cheap and nasty, short and dirty, way of dealing with people one doesn't know and doesn't much care about. It disposes of the problem of getting rid of such people as quickly as possible. There is an air of prejudice about it, as if to say – 'These people are used to getting short shrift, so let's perpetuate that.' It seems like what I consider a third-rate therapy for what they seem to consider third-rate people. I am sure the accountants and the insurance people and the empiricist researchers and the health service would all love it for their various institutional reasons, but I can't see how a human being would love it.

If we want to combine cheapness and accessibility with a proper regard for the length of time a person might need, let us teach co-counselling on a wider basis, rather than rushing to the solution of shorter and shorter periods of professional counselling.

References

Barkham, Michael (1989) 'Exploratory therapy in two-plus-one sessions', *British Journal of Psychotherapy*, 6(1): 81–100.

Butcher, James and Koss, Mary (1978) 'Research on brief and crisis-oriented therapies', in S. Garfield and A. Bergin (eds), *Handbook of Psychotherapy and Behavior Change* (2nd edn). New York: John Wiley.

Dryden, Windy and Barkham, Michael (1990) 'The two-plus-one model: a dialogue', *Counselling Psychology Review*, 5(4): 5–18.

Garfield, S. (1977) in H. Strupp (chair) 'Short-term psychotherapy for whom?' Symposium presented at the annual meeting of the Society for Psychotherapy Research, Madison, Wisconsin.

Kopp, Sheldon (1977) *Back to One*. Palo Alto: Science & Behavior.

Strupp, Hans (1978) 'Psychotherapy research and practice: an overview', in S. Garfield and A. Bergin (eds), *Handbook of Psychotherapy and Behavior Change* (2nd edn). New York: John Wiley.

Ursano, R.J. and Dressler, D.M. (1974) 'Brief vs long-term psychotherapy: a treatment decision', *Journal of Nervous and Mental Disease*, 159: 164–71.

6 Client resistance

I read somewhere that client resistance in counselling stems from the client not wanting to do what the counsellor explicitly or implicitly wants him/her to do. Do you agree with this view?

Michael Jacobs

The term 'resistance', like some others in counselling terminology, carries the unfortunate and mistaken notion that clients are wilfully difficult and unco-operative, and liable to engage in a battle with the counsellor. ('Confrontation' is another term with similar connotations.) It is easy to forget that the client has come voluntarily, and wants to feel better! I want to stress from the outset that if 'resistance' describes some blocking in communication, which there often is between a counsellor and a client, it is always for a *good* reason (not a *bad* one), and that the reason needs to be understood. I also want to stress that resistance takes place just as much within people as it does between people (and again for good reasons), inasmuch as we become alienated from ourselves. Finally, I need to make it clear that resistance as a counselling phenomenon is not confined to clients but also appears, with equal frequency in counsellors.

Resistance tends to occur because people in some way sense the presence in them of an idea, feeling, thought or phantasy that they also experience as impossible for them to allow in themselves or to express to another without the equal or even greater threat of anxiety, fear, guilt or shame. Sometimes either the original feeling or the secondary fear, and sometimes both, exist below the surface of awareness, with no recognition at all of 'resisting'. In other cases someone is aware of a sense of being blocked, although not always sure what is wrong. Sometimes the person is fully aware of both the feeling and the secondary fear of guilt, and because of that awareness unable to voice either to another person. Resistance may take the form of a thought block, emotional numbness, deliberate or involuntary changing of the subject, and other forms of verbal expression or even action (such as missing sessions). Counsellors come to recognize that such forms of resistance are just as present in themselves when they function as counsellors as they are in their clients.

The traditional view of resistance is that the client (consciously and/or unconsciously) needs to keep both the threat (of anxiety, guilt etc.) and the unexpressed thought or emotion from emerging in the relationship to, or in communication with the counsellor. In some sense that is true of all types of resistance, whatever their origin. But the common view is that such feelings or thoughts have their origins either in the client's life outside the session, or in the client's experience of the counselling session. This view suggests that the counsellor has done nothing to provoke the client's resistance, except by legitimately pursuing appropriate therapeutic aims. It is the client who resists this task. The statement in the question above is correct inasmuch as the counsellor explicitly (or implicitly) enters into a contract with the client, in which the counsellor offers to help the client pursue self-reflection, behaviour change and insight. As the client begins to face working through anxiety-provoking or guilt-ridden thoughts and feelings in order to achieve these goals, it is possible (some would say inevitable) that avoidance of the anxiety and guilt will take precedence over therapeutic gains, and that the client will begin to show signs of resisting both the counsellor's expertise and the counselling process. Given that many clients are eager to resolve their difficulties, such blocks may be thought only to come from unconscious forces, sabotaging the client's progress. For example, traditional psychoanalytic terminology might speak of the threat to the 'gain from illness' paradoxically leading to a temporary 'flight into health'.

Such views of resistance, while important and sometimes valid, are not sufficient. They simplistically assume that counsellors know what they are doing, that they are carrying out their task relatively free from error, and that their therapeutic motives are pure. What this interesting question also suggests is that the client may resist doing what the counsellor expects of the client, when the counsellor's expectation is a false or mistaken one, and when the counsellor is behaving in an anti-therapeutic fashion.

Counsellors have their own resistances to clients. One counsellor, for example, may find it impossible to accept a client's angry feelings when expressed towards himself; another may have a personal block about permitting the expression of intimacy and fondness; another may have a therapeutic zeal which is geared more to the counsellor's sense of achievement than the client's. Many authorities (particularly within the psychodynamic tradition) recognize that counsellors have personal barriers, and that these interfere with their ability to understand, empathize and enter into a therapeutic relationship with some of their clients.

What such authorities less often recognize is that a client's resistance may be to the problems which the counsellor brings into the session from outside, or which the counsellor creates in the therapeutic relationship. Some resistance may be 'counsellogenic'! One notable exception to this lack of recognition is the American analyst Robert Langs. He sometimes appears to be suggesting that clients spend most of their time trying to correct, and therefore resisting the crass responses of their therapists (Smith, 1991).

It is vital for counsellors to acknowledge (which initially can only take the form of an intellectual acceptance of the possibility) that they will themselves unconsciously force their clients into a type of resistance which is entirely appropriate, because the client has to defend herself or himself against the actual harm or potential damage towards which the counsellor is leading the client.

To illustrate this, let us take a single situation, and reflect on it from the different perspectives which I have already outlined. A client starts the session by saying that she has nothing to say this week. She falls into a silence, which the counsellor experiences as being most uncomfortable. The counsellor suggests that the client is perhaps feeling uncomfortable, not just about having nothing to say, but because if she began to talk, it might be too upsetting. The client nods, and a tear trickles down her cheek. She had forgotten, she says, that in the middle of the week she heard bad news from her parents which had really upset her, but which she quickly got over. In this instance the client experiences resistance to talking about a situation, because of the risk of feeling upset again. She resists this both earlier in the week in herself and now with the counsellor, temporarily blocking the therapeutic process of enabling painful feelings to be given fuller expression.

Now looking at a similar situation from a different perspective, the same client starts the session by saying that she has nothing to say this week. The counsellor uses the initial silence to think back to the last session. He realizes (partly because it came up in supervision) that the last time they met he had not said anything in response to this client when she told him about bad news which she had had from her parents. She said this situation had upset her, and that she had quickly got over it. While the counsellor thought that he had been correct in allowing the client to put the subject to one side (to collude for therapeutic reasons with the resistance) he had since recognized that the client had really wanted him to help her acknowledge the pain. He had in fact said nothing. Her resistance in this session is in direct response to his failure last time. He had implicitly wanted to encourage her to avoid the pain. She now expresses (by giving up on her counsellor) her resistance to her counsellor giving up on her.

A third, yet more difficult situation might have arisen had this counsellor, after giving rise to the resistance in the first place (through his own shortcomings), then compounded the error with injustice. It is not unknown for counsellors, faced with a silent client, to accuse them (as clients often perceive it) of being resistant. And if the counsellor suggests prematurely that the client is resistant, rather than acknowledging his own error, the client will probably become even more resistant, caught in a vicious circle of the counsellor's making.

Caricatures of counselling often portray the counsellor as confronting clients with their resistance to anger, tears, sexual feelings, the transference, etc. In real life counsellors need to understand that resistance is a universal phenomenon, present in everyone, and is often a way of responding to a situation which is quite warranted: either because what the client faces are feelings which would otherwise be too difficult to take on board, or because the client is legitimately telling the counsellor that he or she is wrong, inept or even damaging. It is probably not a bad rule to make the starting point of any experience of resistance a silent enquiry into the attitude or behaviour of the counsellor, before assuming that resistance has its origin in the client. Even if in the end it turns out to be more the client's difficulty than the counsellor's, clients find it much easier to accept their own contribution to the sense of counselling becoming blocked when they recognize that their counsellor is ready to own the possibility of their own error, oversight or pressure on the client.

In summary, the question poses a view with which I do agree, but for reasons which may not be immediately obvious in the way the statement is phrased. Counsellor expectations are a major explanation of resistance: but counsellor expectations are not always therapeutic. And when the client resists what is anti-therapeutic, counsellors are being told they have a lot more to learn.

Reference

Smith, D.L. (1991) *Hidden Conversations: An Introduction to Communicative Psychoanalysis*. London: Routledge.

7 The ending phase of counselling

*What signs do clients give to indicate that they are
moving into the ending phase of counselling?
Under what conditions should I as counsellor raise
this issue with clients of working towards
termination and how should I best approach it?*

Dave Mearns

Frankly, I do not understand how counsellors *can* know when it is
appropriate to raise the issue of working towards an ending.
Certainly there can be an observable process whereby the client's
fear, confusion, tension and disintegration give way to greater
hope, clarity, comfort and integration, however, within the
counselling process there are also *plateaux* representing times when
the client's life catches up with the changes which have been
happening within the self. Even though the development process
within the client's self is not complete it is perfectly possible to
have an ending at that phase of the process so long as it is perfectly
clear to the client that they can restart whenever they want.

In practice, it is the parameters of the counselling agency which
are most important in dictating endings. Apart from private practice work there are few counselling contexts which nowadays offer
a client-centred service with respect to endings. Indeed, some agencies dictate the ending before the start of counselling with the
expectation being aired that 'We shall have up to a maximum of
six/nine/twelve sessions.' Time-limited counselling is likely to
create an ending at the first plateau of the therapeutic process.
However, such a policy allows the agency to spread its counselling
resources more widely.

The expectations which client, counsellor and agency hold about
the extensiveness of a counselling process will influence the time of
ending. If the counselling is defined in narrow terms, like helping
the client to negotiate the depression phase of a transition, then the
counselling is going to end much earlier than if the contract also
allowed for support in re-evaluating life and internalizing the
consequences of the transition. Most often I am working in
counselling contracts which are even broader and deeper, where the
client may be making a fundamental development of personality to
the point where significant self-acceptance is achieved. Logically,

the depth and breadth of the counselling process is dictated by the lowest common denominator of the expectations of client, counsellor and agency.

The 'signs' which clients give to suggest a movement into the ending phase of counselling depend largely upon the breadth and depth of the counselling process envisaged. If the counselling is restricted to supporting the client through a difficult phase in life then the ending phase might be indicated by the client's reduction or control of his or her *depression* combined with the beginnings of *hope* for the future. On the other hand, if the counselling is being defined in terms of personality development then an ending phase might be indicated by the client becoming less *driven* by elements of his/her pathology. While some of these elements of his/her pathology will actually have changed, most will still be around but will have lost much of their power through the awareness the client has gained. The client will also be exhibiting a significant reduction in *fear* about the past and the present, though he/she may still be fearful of the future life changes which could be a consequence of the therapeutic process. A parallel development is that the client will become less *constrained* in his or her functioning, moving more freely from one way of being to another. These consequences of reduced pathology, fear and constraint bring with them an enormous experience of personal power and may release considerable energy for action. Sometimes clients need help with the early phase of that release because they are unfamiliar with their own power.

One of the clearest indicators of the ending process, but one which should not be expected in every case, is evidence of the client's *self-acceptance*. I prick up my ears when I hear a client saying something like: 'Maybe I am not so bad after all', or 'I am certainly not all good but I don't feel so bad about being bad!' or 'I guess I did the best I could.'

It is difficult to raise the question of ending without the client hearing this as a *suggestion*. This is not such a problem in processes which have run a longer course and have resulted in greater empowerment of the client as well as increased mutuality in the counselling relationship, but in shorter counselling contracts where the same development of the relationship has not occurred the client may defer too much to the judgment of the counsellor. I have spent much time asking clients about their experiences of counselling and have developed a fair scepticism of the extent to which the counsellor is aware of how the client actually experiences the counsellor. The counsellor may be saying 'I wonder if we should think about whether to begin to end or not?' and the client may be feeling 'He wants to end!' I try to voice *all* that I am experiencing on those rare occasions when I raise the question of working towards an ending. Such a statement is likely to include my uncertainty and confusion since I am not at all confident about making judgments on endings. It may also include a comment on fears I have about raising the question at all. Usually the statement is followed by quite a bit of dialogue on the various feelings and thoughts which the client and myself are experiencing at that moment. This emphasis on my own congruence and my encouragement of the client's congruence is the best safeguard that I have against the client misinterpreting my statement or over-reacting to it.

I treat 'endings' as part of an ongoing process. I never make an ending absolute unless in exceptional circumstances when that is precisely what the client wants and needs in order to experience the full extent of his/her responsibility for himself/herself. In my practice I have a definite rule which keeps the process open even after an ending. I make it clear to the client that they may come back at any time for reviews or restarts. In that event they will be able to engage me *immediately*, with no question of being put on a waiting list or told that I do not have room for them. This policy is part of my continuing commitment to the client even after what may appear to be an ending. I have found this policy to be crucial in many cases in the past when the client later realized that our 'ending' was in fact a *plateau* in the overall process. My counselling practice has to be designed to cope with this degree of flexibility in that I must ensure that I am never counselling to full capacity, always allowing space for re-entries. Only once in the past, when three former clients simultaneously wanted to start again, did I find that this caused any difficulty whatsoever. Even then, the increased workload lasted only for a few weeks.

Towards the end of even a successful counselling process there lurks one grave danger. Because our culture is bedevilled by fairytales whereby endings are not merely 'happy' but 'happy ever after', the client and indeed the counsellor may be shaken by the fact that the client is not feeling at all happy – indeed, he or she may be somewhat depressed. The client at the end of a successful counselling process will have *lost* a lot. He or she will have lost a set of assumptions and a self-concept which, although limiting of his or her existence, had also served to *define* that existence. This sense of loss may be intensified by the fact that the client had always presumed that once through this difficulty, life would be like the fairytales. This was well described by one client during a 'review' meeting following what we both thought had been an ending:

One of the most lonely times was when the depression of reality moved in. I had lost something. I had lost something I thought I never wanted. It had been a burden to me throughout my life but now I did not have it any more and that was scary in itself. Also I did not have the hope of what life would be like without it. Reality can be a bleak prospect when you are used to a diet of fairytales.

PART TWO

ISSUES OF MATCHING IN COUNSELLING

---

8 Advising on the most suitable counselling arena

When clients are referred to me I am sometimes uncertain whether they are best suited to individual counselling, couples work or group counselling. What guidelines do you suggest I use to help me make a decision?

Mark Aveline

The allocation of clients to type of therapy is not an exact science; therapist skill, therapy availability, type of problem and client preference set the parameters for an important decision, both in terms of outcome and use of resource. The decision should be considered on two levels: general suitability for counselling and specific suitability for a particular approach.

General suitability for counselling

Even before deciding on a particular approach, the counsellor needs to assess the utility and safety for the particular client of their embarking on counselling. The information that is required comes from (a) the referral letter, (b) history volunteered by the client and then amplified, deepened and modified in conversation and (c) the counsellor's experience of the client as a person with unique but informative ways of reacting to the encounter of assessment. David Malan (1979), a former psychoanalyst at the Tavistock Clinic and pioneer of brief psychotherapy, advocates assessment on four levels: psychiatrically, psychodynamically, psychotherapeutically and practically. In addition, the counsellor must take care of the assessment itself so that, as rapport deepens with the client, it can yield the required information *and* take care of the client to guard against the assessment being damaging. Malan was assessing for suitability for interpretative psychotherapy but his four levels set out a framework of broad utility. What do his levels mean? This account draws on Malan's work and the author's experience.

It is important to be as sure as one can be that the client is not suffering from an autonomous severe mental disorder or physical illness which can be treated more expeditiously or effectively with medication or other intervention than with counselling. *Psychiatrically*, the common conditions that need to be excluded are severe depression and psychosis; suspicious features are pessimistic or persecutory perceptions that are out of line with the person's situation and recognized as such by those closest to the sufferer (when the perceptions are treated as normal and held to despite all evidence to the contrary, the person is said to lack 'insight' and the symptoms are deemed to be delusional), alteration in physiological dimensions such as loss of appetite and weight, a pattern of improvement in mood as the day wears on, general inability to laugh, loss of interest in sex and personal interests, and suicidal intent. The presence of a major change of mental state that cannot be easily accounted for in terms of what has gone before in the person's life and which is out of character suggests that psychiatric assessment might be of value. Anti-depressive or anti-psychotic medication is rarely a total solution for personal problems but they may avert tragic outcomes and raise the person to the point where they are able to explore psychological issues productively.

Continuing the psychiatric theme, impulsivity and drug and alcohol dependence militate against the collaborative work towards solutions that is the hallmark of counselling. For the work to proceed, it should be possible to *formulate the client's problems in psychological terms* and *reach consensus* that there are psychological aspects to the problems. A clash of models as when the client considers him- or herself to be simply and passively ill and the counsellor is proposing an active model of personal responsibility does no good to either party. In assessing *psychodynamically*, Malan means making a dynamic hypothesis that identifies conscious and unconscious conflicts which are active in the present problem and will undoubtedly feature in the therapy. The hypothesis draws together aetiological factors, those that are predisposing, precipitating and perpetuating, and tries to answer the often difficult question of why has this person developed this problem at this point in their life? Whatever the preferred explanatory model, be it psychodynamic, cognitive-behavioural or systems based, the *hypothesis* must be based on evidence in the client's situation, be appropriate to the counsellor's way of working and be useful in advancing the client's understanding. An hypothesis is like a map which indicates the way traversed to reach the client's location in their life and depicts likely future directions and reactions. If it is not possible to begin to make such an hypothesis, counselling may well be inappropriate.

Counselling is no easy option and clients need to be *willing to face their feelings* and *look beneath the surface*. Particularly in longer-term work where the goal is personal change rather than the equally valid but less ambitious goal of helping a client through a crisis or to make a decision, the client needs to be *motivated to change*. Furthermore, can the client form a sufficient *therapeutic alliance* for the work? This means the adult-to-adult alliance between client and counsellor that enables the therapy to continue when the going gets rough; the alliance requires a sufficiency of trust so that a 'good-enough' image of the counsellor can be maintained despite negative transference. A history of inability to form trusting relationships and adverse reactions in the form of suspicion, withdrawal or fragmentation of thought during the exploration of assessment bodes ill for the success of counselling. Thinking *psychotherapeutically* means assessing the client's strengths and his ability to cope with challenges, including that of counselling itself. A key dimension is *ego strength* which is assessed both through the history of how the person has coped with developmental stages and stressful events (extreme reactions or collapse suggest low ego strength) and how the client reacts to interpretations or other awareness-expanding interventions during the assessment. Low ego-strength should be matched by caution on the part of the counsellor, generally in the direction of working more slowly and at lesser depth.

People do not develop in the way that they do by chance. A person's defences, however inappropriate and out of date now, were needed ways of coping with difficult situations in the past and should not be forced to yield, except as new strengths develop. The assessing counsellor has responsibility for gauging *potential gains and losses* through therapy and discussing these with the client so that she can make an *informed choice* about proceeding. Therapy frequently disrupts the status quo and in so doing opens the way to change, but the new state may not be acceptable to the parties concerned; the marriage, occupation, dependence on parents and balance of interests may all be questioned. Often there is an *auspicious time* (*Kairos*) in a person's life to take stock and alter established ways; counselling then may be especially helpful. Conversely, there are times when it is better to defer counselling or leave well alone. A case for *deferment* can be, for example, during pregnancy when the focus of the mother's attention is predominantly and necessarily inwards; raising major external questions during this period through therapy can significantly increase stress. *Leaving well alone* may be the right course when the counsellor judges that the client's inner world is so fragile that any change would be for the worse or that the client has insufficient personal resources to make major developmental moves. Someone who has not developed an independent life by their 50s is unlikely to do so.

Assessing *practically* means asking oneself the question: do I have the requisite skill, time and interest to counsel this client? If not, who does?

Specific suitability for a particular approach

The justification for detailed assessment is twofold: selecting out those for whom counselling would be inappropriate and matching therapy to client. The last point supposes that a choice is available as is only proper when different problems respond to different interventions. Matching takes account of duration effect, treatment specificity, locus, the client's readiness to benefit, complexity of problems, counsellor compatibility and availability.

Research suggests that much of the benefit from psychotherapy accrues in the first few sessions. A closer reading of the *duration effect* literature demonstrates a differential effect: morale and self-esteem are boosted within approximately four sessions, symptoms show the greatest reduction in the four to sixteen-session range but improvement in quality of relationships does not show till upwards of twelve sessions with, in my experience, peaks at 25, 50 and 150 sessions. This generalization gives some guidance when planning how long a therapy a client will need. Thus a person who has been badly abused will be slow to develop trust and need more time than someone facing a recent trauma whose personality is robust.

Therapies have *specific effects* and aptitudes. Individual counselling affords psychological space and time to explore personal history and individual problems. Intensity both in terms of depth and speed can be fine-tuned to individual need. I tend to recommend individual dynamic work when the person's problems stem from their view of themselves and intra-psychic conflicts that they want to consider in light of their history. Cognitive-behavioural work fits naturally with those whose perspective is limited to symptoms and who want to be directed in their therapy. In addition, cognitive-behavioural therapy has clear advantage in the treatment of phobias and obsessive-compulsive disorder. Couple work addresses a living relationship wherein people show their strengths and vulnerabilities and play out their conflicts. Change achieved here has an immediate benefit. Clients may be stuck in interactive patterns that can only be freed up by engaging the key other. The same is true of family therapy. Groups are a splendid setting in which the client can learn about how he interacts, sees others and is seen. It is a laboratory in which risks can be taken and change made. Groups can provide a supportive 'family' for clients with long-term needs and dilute the impact of those whose paranoia, fragility or dependence would be overwhelming in individual counselling.

Where the problem is *located* helps to decide the therapy. Intrapsychic problems and problematic attitudes to self which do not involve another person in a current intimate relationship or where that other is unwilling to be involved suggest individual therapy. When the problem is located within a particular relationship such as a couple, and that is the problem that the client wants to resolve, focus the therapy on the couple. Group counselling is indicated for recurrent maladaptive relationship patterns or where an important therapeutic element of the counselling is sharing some experience in common e.g. cancer, sexual abuse, phobias and eating disorder.

Finally there is an interaction between the *client's readiness to benefit* and *complexity of problems*, and the *counsellor's compatibility* and *availability*. Consideration needs to be given to providing different forms of counselling in sequence and, in complex cases, referring on for more specialized therapy. The optimum intervention might be a group but first the client might need to work through individually a particular aspect of their history or develop sufficient trust in order to be able to benefit from the sharing and exposure of a group. The counsellor should consider if the counselling would be advanced by matching for age and gender and how suitable he or she is on these dimensions. Is there sufficient harmony of outlook to be compatible? Does the counsellor have the skills (and supervision) that will be needed and, once started, can the counselling be seen through to its conclusion? It is not ethical to open up major issues without providing space and time for resolution.

These selection guidelines should not be read as absolutes. How clients engage with counselling varies enormously. It is important that clients participate in the decision about which form of counselling they should embark on. Their preference, sometimes informed by trial sessions, should be taken into account but, again, not as an absolute. In counselling, what a person fears most may be the most beneficial approach.

References

Aveline, M.O. (1980) 'Making a psychodynamic formulation', *Bulletin, Royal College of Psychiatrists* (December): 192–3.

Malan, D. (1979) *Individual Psychotherapy and the Science of Psychodynamics.* London: Butterworths.

9 Women counselling women

Some of my fellow trainees believe that only
women should counsel women, but I am against
this position which I consider to be separatist.
What are your views on this topic?

Jocelyn Chaplin

This is a very complex issue which for me does not have simple single answers. First, I do believe strongly that if a woman asks specifically to see a woman counsellor, that request should be granted. I have heard professionals talking as if 'they know best' and even deliberately not providing a client with what she asks for. This may stem from a theory that people actually *need* the opposite of what they ask for: for example, a man is what she really needs if she has deliberately asked for a woman. Perhaps she's afraid of dealing with her father 'stuff'. I am horrified by this approach which I feel does not respect the client as an equal human being, which is so important in feminist as well as other therapeutic approaches.

Second, I do think that there are a number of good reasons why many women prefer to see female counsellors and why many women 'do better' with women counsellors. There are some situations in which it might be more obvious than others; for example, counselling after rape by a man. Certainly in the immediate aftermath of such an experience most women will need support and empathy from other women. However, there might be, in the future, a time when it would be helpful for that person to see a man counsellor and express all those feelings of rage more directly.

For many women coming into counselling at all can be a very daunting experience, telling some strange 'authority figure' all about our innermost feelings and thoughts. For many this would be easier with another woman. They would perhaps feel safer and trust more quickly. They might be more likely to feel that the counsellor understands them. Although there will also be issues of class and race which can create problems in these initial stages. A very middle-class woman could be more intimidating to a working class client than a working-class man might be. The problem is often essentially one of power difference.

As we live in a deeply patriarchal society, men are still seen as the 'superior' sex underneath the surface of all our protestations to the contrary. The counselling world is a very female world in many ways and most of the men involved in it are sensitive and emotionally aware. Because of these facts, counsellors often underestimate the power of patriarchy deep in the psyche of even the newest of new men *and* of the most articulate of feminists. So people are already coming into counselling with a whole set of expectations and deep attitudes around gender. For most of us, men have been the most respected and important authority figures in our lives, even if women have seemed more powerful. Somehow, the things that a man says have been listened to just that little bit more attentively!

So, for a woman, having a male counsellor can too easily simply reproduce all the inequalities she has experienced every day outside. Counselling could even de-power her by being yet another time when a man is in charge or even telling her what she thinks. Of course, the more non-directive the man is, the less of a problem this might be. But even non-directive men counsellors who feel they are being equal are not necessarily going to be seen that way by the client. And even the most sensitive of men have not had the experience of living inside a woman's body or growing up as a girl in a patriarchal society.

However, third, I must stress that there can be a place for women being counselled by men. Generally I feel that this might be most useful in a later stage of counselling, after the initial problems have been worked through and greater self-understanding has been achieved. When a woman has built up a reasonably strong ego or sense of self then she might be ready to work with a man. Some women find it easier to express anger, for example, with men than with women. Woman-to-woman counselling can become too cosy and not address some of the more negative feelings that might come up in the transference. It might be easier to work with a man when dealing with father issues, for example, although female counsellors can become our 'fathers' just as easily as they can become our 'mothers'. Often transference is less affected by gender than by other factors such as a need for mothering. Many men can mother and nurture just as effectively as women.

Fourth, there are times in counselling when gender seems unimportant when the interconnection is working really well. It can at times be a deep meeting of souls, and souls ultimately don't have a gender!

I feel that women clients or counsellors who choose to work only with women have many good reasons that need to be respected.

There are times in social change and in our personal journeys when some degree of 'separatism' is necessary to empower ourselves without the worry about relating to members of a 'superior' group. Many people don't realize just how de-powered so many women feel simply being in the presence of men. It is very important in counsellor training that space is given to exploring these issues at as deep a level as possible with honesty and compassion.

Many men, and some women, are threatened by the idea of 'separatism'. They may even have issues around being left out, seeing the all-women group or pair like their families or parents from whom they felt excluded. Some women also have a pattern of rescuing men or wanting everyone to get on and be 'together'. Divisions of any kinds can feel scary for women brought up to emphasize connections and things we have in common rather than things that divide us. Yet there are times when divisions and differences do need to be addressed and acknowledged. They can also be creative, for example, when working in a women's group or with a woman counsellor there can be a freer flow of energy in dance or painting that might be very sexual and too embarrassing to show in front of men.

Indeed, it is probably the area of sexuality that raises the most difficult question about women clients working with men counsellors. Because on the whole, for thousands of years the main connections between men and women have been sexual, many men and some women immediately associate the presence of the opposite gender with sex. They may feel they have to flirt or prove themselves in some way. Or a male counsellor may find himself sexually aroused in the presence of female clients. We all know now just how much abuse there has been over the years of female clients by male therapists and counsellors. It may happen the other way round, but much less often. In sexual encounters men still usually have the power, at least the power to act or not. In good professional counselling feelings of attraction and even sexual arousal can be used without being acted on to help the client explore those issues. But a male counsellor has to be very clear about boundaries and about his own sexuality. Although most male counsellors do have very clear boundaries, there are too many exceptions for some women to want to take the risk. Women are vulnerable enough to male sexuality in the outside world and do not always want to chance feeling even more at risk in the intimate setting of counselling. Even where there are issues around the woman's own sexuality and its problems on a personal level, it is important to remember that there are also social problems. Women are still viewed largely as sex objects by the media and by the male world. And not even all male counsellors have gone as deeply and honestly into their own sexual psyches as they need to in order to be useful to women in this area.

In conclusion I would see a place for 'separatism' but also for some women at appropriate times I see a place for working with men too.

10 Ethnic matching in counselling

How important is it to ethnically match clients and counsellors?

Waseem J. Alladin

The short answer to this complex question is 'It depends'. It may help to consider the rationale behind ethnic matching. When counsellor and client share the same cultural background, empathic understanding and self-disclosure are more easily facilitated. However, most counsellors and counsellor trainers are white, middle-class people whose values and communication styles may differ from those of ethnic minority clients especially those of lower socio-economic status. Thus white counsellors may unwittingly engage in cultural oppression by imposing Western values on ethnic minority clients. Further, ethnic minority clients, because of a historical exposure to, and current experiences of, racism may have a damaged ethnic or racial identity which would hinder the development of a therapeutic alliance with a white counsellor. Thus understanding the client's ethnic or racial identity development is important in cross-cultural counselling.

Ethnicity is a group classification of individuals sharing a unique social and cultural heritage (customs, language, religion) from generation to generation. It therefore follows that ethnicity and race are not necessarily synonymous, though common usage of the term 'race' in the literature really ought to refer specifically to ethnicity or culture. According to Sundberg (1981), culture – a convenient label for knowledge, skills and attitudes that are learned and passed on from one generation to the next – implies a way of life which can become so ingrained that people are not conscious of assumptions they make of themselves and others. In this discussion I will therefore assume that ethnicity and culture are interchangeable terms and focus on black people as one example of an ethnic minority group.

The case for and against ethnic matching

The eurocentric bias in counselling approaches has been highlighted time and again (see Alladin, 1989). Counselling consciously or unconsciously promotes mainstream (majority) cultural values which leads to a culturally encapsulated counsellor and if the client does not share the counsellor's values then the lack of congruence could lead to premature termination by the client or the failure to agree on the goals of counselling. But what's all the fuss about? Surely counselling is a helping process and considerations of colour, ethnicity, religion, etc. should not come into it? Not surprisingly, there are shades of opinion about the desirability of ethnic matching for successful outcome in counselling.

Let us first consider somewhat extreme views which insist on ethnic matching or reject outright any need for ethnic matching. One extreme view is that the white counsellor cannot possibly counsel the 'Black psyche' and would merely perpetuate the 'colonial master–slave' relationship. More accurately, a white counsellor who has not developed awareness of cultural issues, denies the presence of racism and the impact of colonization and is unable to empathize with the oppression that many black clients feel in a dominant white society, is obviously not going to develop a helping relationship. Such a counsellor should not be surprised by 'premature' termination or blame the client for 'lack of motivation' or even a presumed 'inability to benefit from counselling'.

A strict and inflexible insistence on ethnic matching of client and counsellor risks a danger of segregation with white clients being seen only by white counsellors and black clients being seen only by black counsellors. This not only clashes with the principle that counsellors should offer services to all citizens but is contrary to the notion of generic counsellor training. Matching black clients with black counsellors assumes that the black counsellor necessarily shares the same values and ignores possible class differences. Further, as Kareem (1992) warns, matching done purely on the basis of race or colour can imprison both the counsellor and the client in their own racial and cultural identity. It also diminishes the human element which must be an integral part of all professional encounters.

To contrast our discussion with another extreme view, consider Patterson (1978: 133) who rejects the principles and practices of cross-culturalism:

> The role of counseling and psychotherapy is to facilitate the development of self-actualization in clients. Cultures can be evaluated in terms of their contribution to the self-actualization of their members. The major conditions for the development of self-actualizing persons are known, and must be present in counseling and psychotherapy as practiced with any client regardless of culture . . . . The problems of practicing counseling or psychotherapy in others' cultures are viewed as problems of implementing these conditions. Certain characteristics of

clients which present obstacles to the implementation of the conditions are associated with certain cultures. Until cultural changes lead to change in these characteristics, counseling or psychotherapy will be difficult and in some cases impossible with certain clients from certain cultures. Structuring and client education and training may change client expectations and make therapy possible. In any case, however, to accede to client expectations, abandoning methods which have been demonstrated to be related to self-actualization as an outcome of counseling or psychotherapy, is to abandon self-actualization as the goal, and to accept goals which are often inconsistent with self-actualization.

This 'colour- and culture-blind' view is naive and denies the real world in which people live. As Draguns (1989) notes, Patterson's critique rests on several misunderstandings of cross-cultural counselling in theory and in practice. The goal of cross-cultural counselling is not to change the culture but to enable change to take place in the client. Cross-cultural counsellors also reject the notion that whatever does not aim at self-actualization is not counselling. Counselling, Draguns suggests, starts with distress that the client cannot alleviate or with a problem he or she cannot solve.

In counselling the culturally different client, the counsellor may unwittingly engage in cultural oppression, that is, the unconscious imposition of mainstream cultural values on to the client. Any counsellor should be able to counsel effectively irrespective of ethnicity. In other words, all counsellors should acquire cross-cultural competencies so that they can deal effectively with culturally different clients.

Others take the view that the client's preferences for a white or black counsellor should always be respected. In principle this seems commendable. However, a risk is that this preference can sometimes hide avoidance both on the part of the client who requests it and the counsellor who accedes to it, if the reasons for it are not explored honestly.

The benefits of developing cross-cultural competence

The same-ethnicity counsellor–client dyad has both advantages and disadvantages which vary according to the theoretical background of the counsellor. For example, Tyler, Sussewell and Williams-McCoy (1985) consider the various pairings of white and ethnic minority counsellors and clients (see also Lago and Thompson, 1989). A black client can have a therapeutically helpful and unique learning experience from working with a white counsellor if his or her racial/ethnic uniqueness can be valued and appreciated without condescension. The white counsellor, in turn, can gain a far deeper and less intellectually contained sense of the pain and destructiveness of discrimination, of the ways in which counsellors may use their theories to rationalize their prejudices, and of the strengths the black client can bring to his or her struggle with racism and with him- or herself.

Research on ethnic matching

Pedersen, Fukuyama and Heath (1989) conclude that the findings from research on client counselling preferences for same-race counsellors are mixed and raise more questions than answers. Some reasons for this are inadequate research methodologies and measures and the limitations of using a narrowly defined concept of 'race'. To encompass the complexities of cross-cultural relationships other variables such as the client's racial identity, social class and counselling style preferences need to be considered. Since the research literature on ethnic matching is mixed, the safest conclusion at present is that ethnic matching can reduce premature termination rates but does not seem to make a significant difference to therapeutic outcome. Case examples from counselling practice, on the other hand confirm, at the very least, the need to be aware of racial and cultural issues and to accommodate different world-views. As Thomas and Althen (1985) put it (in the context of counselling foreign students, for example), to be effective with foreign clients, counsellors must learn to adapt their counselling styles and their expectations to accommodate the differing world-views and cultural value orientations of their foreign clients.

The importance of ethnic or racial identity in cross-cultural counselling

The white counsellor (and the black client) may stereotype each other and be surprised by an oppressive silence or even open hostility. Edwards (1983) stresses that a general disposition shared by some black people is that personal problems should not be discussed outside the family: 'Never tell your business to strangers; black people have to be careful about who they talk to.' Edwards notes that some black clients may have knee-jerk hostile reactions which include statements like: 'That's none of your business . . . . What do you want to know that for? . . . How would I know? I mind my own business,' and cautions against interpreting the client's responses in a literal, concrete way. The counsellor should view such reticence about self-disclosure and/or hostility as signals of anxieties and as styles of self-protective armour. On the other hand, to react defensively, Edwards (1983) warns, is to give legitimacy to the client's need for self-protection. In these eventualities, it is essential that the counsellor use a model of racial identity to understand the blocks to the relationship.

Helms (1984) outlined a model of racial identity, focusing on the dynamics of cross-racial dyads so that counsellors can acquire a better understanding of how best to treat the culturally different client. Of course, both counsellor and client have their own ethnic identities. According to Helms (1990) White racial identity development refers to the process through which a White person (here the counsellor) first acknowledges racism, abandons racist attitudes and finally develops a non-racist persona. Black racial identity development refers to the process through which a Black person (here the client) relinquishes negative racial stereotypes that to be Black is 'bad' and inferior to Whites, recognizing the oppressive existence of many Black people under White dominance and finally developing pride in being Black and a more positive self-esteem.

Alladin (1986) has pointed out that in cross-racial dyads, there is a danger of the projection of racism by either party. For example, some clients (and counsellors!) may conveniently and wholly blame racism for all their problems but then refuse to accept any personal responsibility for challenging it or taking steps which could help change their situation. On the other hand, some counsellors (and clients!) may collude in denying racism when it exists for fear of arousing strong emotions. A typical dyad in cross-cultural counselling is that of black client and white counsellor. Jones and Seagull (1983) suggest that in cross-racial interactions it is important for white counsellors to examine feelings aroused, such as white racial guilt for colonial oppression of blacks, countertransference and their need to be powerful. If these issues are not adequately resolved then obviously they would inhibit the development of a therapeutic alliance.

Atkinson and Thompson (1992), in their review of the research on racial, ethnic and cultural variables in counselling, conclude that if race/ethnicity is relevant to the client's problem, then a racially/ethnically similar counsellor who is perceived as expert and trustworthy will exercise greater influence on the client's attitudes.

The problem is, how does the practising counsellor ascertain whether race/ethnicity is relevant to a particular client's problem? One hint from the research literature (see Abramovitz and Murray, 1983) is to look at premature termination rates. A counsellor who finds a disproportionate number of his or her culturally different clients dropping out prematurely can infer that race/ethnicity is relevant and has probably been ignored or mismanaged in counselling.

However, the development of awareness about racism and racial identity, and recognition that cultures different from that of the counsellor are not deviant or deficient, coupled with an understanding of different ways of being (for example, communication styles, world-views, patterns of self-disclosure) can make counselling a truly helping and challenging relationship, irrespective of ethnicity for both counsellor and client.

References and further reading

Abramowitz, S.I. and Murray, J. (1983) 'Race effects in psychotherapy', in J. Murray and P.R. Abramson (eds), *Bias in Psychotherapy*. New York: Praeger.

Alladin, W.J. (1986) 'Clinical psychology and ethnic minorities: an inside view', *Clinical Psychology Forum*, 5: 28–32.

Alladin, W.J. (1989) 'Counselling women and ethnic minorities: problems and prospects', in Special Issue: 'Counselling women and ethnic minorities', *Counselling Psychology Quarterly*, 2(2): 101–4.

Alladin, W.J. (1993) 'Transcultural counselling: theory, research and practice', DCP Reference Library in Clinical Practice, *British Journal of Clinical Psychology*, 32(2).

Atkinson, D.R. and Thompson, C.E. (1992) 'Racial, ethnic, and cultural variables in counseling', in S.D. Brown and R.W. Lent (eds) *Handbook of Counseling Psychology*, (2nd edn). New York: Wiley.

Comas-Diaz, L. and Jacobsen, F.M. (1991) 'Ethnocultural transference and countertransference in the therapeutic dyad', *American Journal of Orthopsychiatry*, 61(3): 392–402.

Draguns, J.D. (1989) 'Dilemmas and choices in cross-cultural counseling: the universal versus the culturally distinctive', in P.B. Pedersen, J.G. Draguns, W.J. Lonner and J.E. Trimble (eds), *Counseling Across Cultures*. Honolulu: University of Hawaii Press.

Edwards, S. (1983) 'Cultural and ethnic perspectives: black cultural attributes and their implications for counseling black clients', in V. D'Andrea and P. Saloavey (eds), *Peer Counseling: Skills and Perspectives*. Palo Alto, CA: Science & Behavior Books.

Helms, J.E. (1984) 'Toward a theoretical explanation of the effects of race on counseling: a Black and White model', *The Counseling Psychologist*, 12(4): 153–65.

Helms, J.E. (1990) *Black and White Racial Identity: Theory, Research and Practice*. Westport, CT: Greenwood Press.

Jones, A. and Seagull, A.A. (1983) 'Dimensions of the relationship between the black client and the white therapist: a theoretical overview', in D.R. Atkinson, G. Morten and D.W. Sue (eds), *Counseling American Minorities: A Cross-Cultural Perspective* (2nd edn). Dubuque, IA: William C. Brown.

Kareem, J. (1992) 'The Nafsiyat Intercultural Therapy Centre', in J. Kareem and R. Littlewood (eds), *Intercultural Therapy: Themes, Interpretations and Practice*. Oxford: Blackwell Scientific Publications.

Lago, C. and Thompson, J. (1989) 'Counselling and race', in W. Dryden, D. Charles-Edwards and R. Woolfe (eds), *Handbook of Counselling in Britain*. London: Routledge.

Patterson, C.H. (1978) 'Cross-cultural or intercultural psychotherapy', *International Journal for the Advancement of Counselling*, 1: 231–48.

Pedersen, P.B., Fukuyama, M. and Heath, A. (1989) 'Client, counselor and contextual variables in multicultural counseling', in P.B. Pedersen, J.G. Draguns, W.J. Lonner and J.E. Trimble (eds), *Counseling Across Cultures*. Honolulu: University of Hawaii Press.

Sundberg, N.D. (1981) 'Cross-cultural counseling and psychotherapy: a research overview', in A.J. Marsella and P.B. Pedersen (eds), *Cross-cultural Counseling and Psychotherapy: Foundations, Evaluation and Cultural Considerations*. New York: Pergamon Press.

Sue, D.W. and Sue, D. (1990) *Counseling the Culturally Different* (2nd edn). New York: Wiley.

Thomas, K. and Althen, G. (1989) 'Counseling foreign students', in P.B. Pedersen, J.G. Draguns, W.J. Lonner and J.E. Trimble (eds), *Counseling Across Cultures*. Honolulu: University of Hawaii Press.

Tyler, F.B., Sussewell, D.R. and Williams-McCoy, J. (1985) 'Ethnic validity in psychotherapy', in G.R. Dudley and M.L. Rawlins (eds) Special Issue: Psychotherapy with ethnic minorities. *Psychotherapy*, 22(22) Supplement: 311–20.

11 Trainee counsellors' clients

*Should counsellors in training work only with
selected clients or should we see anyone who
'comes in the door'?*

Michael Carroll

There are counsellor trainers who argue that it does no harm to
beginners to 'throw them in the deep end' and allow them to see
whatever clients 'come through the door'. They contend that all
counsellors, beginners and those qualified or experienced, find
their own level with the client in front of them and do what they
are able to do. They recount examples where experienced counsellors have given up and the enthusiasm, interest, concern and
care of the beginner have helped bring about unforeseen change in
the client. They point out that numerous clients would not be seen,
either because of waiting lists or the client's lack of money, if they
were not allocated to beginners and, after all, 'some counselling is
better than no counselling'.

These are not arguments to be dismissed lightly, even though I
intend arguing the opposite, that counsellors in training should see
only selected clients and that these clients be chosen with some care
to reflect the experience of the trainee. There may well be a place
for beginners seeing clients they would not normally see because of
specific circumstances, but I would prefer not to consider this as
the norm, nor indeed call it counselling. It could be a supportive
friendship or a buddy system or a limited space to allow the client
to talk about issues. In a Youth Counselling Agency in the USA
we trained 'peer counsellors' to work with young people. These
'peers' were aged from 15 to 18 and were given a basic 10-week
training in Reality Therapy. They then worked with the qualified
staff as co-counsellors of the teenagers coming to the centre. They
did enormous good and often formed better 'working alliances'
with the clients than did the qualified counsellors, the clients identifying with them more readily. In this context, and with the structures mentioned, they saw quite disturbed young people, and did
marvellous work.

Most professions gradually introduce the learner to more
difficult aspects of the profession. A beginner surgeon does not
start with a triple by-pass operation nor does a pilot's first lesson

in flying demand a solo flight across the Atlantic. Social workers are not set adrift in their first placement with a dysfunctional family which has a history of 'devouring' helpers. Allowing beginners gradual access to more difficult situations helps them learn gradually and build up a repertoire of knowledge and skills in an easier area before tackling the more difficult. Most professions, counselling included, tend to have more complex areas that require greater experience, and often further learning, before the practitioner is ready to engage with it.

I base the argument that trainees ought to be gradually introduced to more difficult clients on three premises. First, trainees move through stages in their development and these stages are characterized by extra skills and increased abilities. Second, clients present with problems/issues that range from mild to very severe, and therefore require different levels of counsellor experience. Third, supervision is the inbuilt monitor for helping trainees understand their strengths and limitations and gauge the level of their abilities with clients. I will look at these three in more detail.

The stages through which trained counsellors move

Much work has been done in the past few years on the stages trainees go through in their journey to becoming professionals. Stoltenberg and Delworth (1987) have put forward an interesting three-level model outlining this process, leading towards what they call the 'master-counsellor'. The counsellor moves from novice to experienced practitioner. Their underlying argument is that the counsellor in training is able to think, feel and act differently at each stage. They outline the process in three levels. At Level 1 trainees focus primarily on self, rather than on the other person (the client). They watch themselves work, searching for the right way ahead. Their motivation is based on a desire to help, with little awareness of the underlying, and often unconscious, reasons for counselling others. And they are dependent, at this stage, on the experts, the authorities, for their methods, theories and techniques. One of my supervisees, who was at this level, remarked during a supervision session that she 'was so busy listening to herself listening to the client that she did not hear what he was saying'.

The Level 2 trainee moves from self to client. Here he/she is able to enter the world of the client as distinct from their own world, understand and appreciate the differences between individuals, and begin to both see and work with the complexities of the counselling situation. Some confusion may come with accepting this complexity, and the trainee is often unsure of his or her own motivation for wanting to counsel. There is more independence in working with clients, the trainee now monitoring and sifting the supervision session rather than accepting it as the authoritative way of counselling. An example of the Level 2 trainee was the supervisee who recounted her first session with a new client. The story was horrendous, and about 5 minutes into the facts of the situation, the trainee burst into tears and fled the room. She was quite overcome, and had closely identified with the client. There was still no clear distinction between herself and the people coming for help.

Level 3 trainees are aware of self and others, how the two are distinct, and how they merge. They usually have a strong theoretical base to their work, which guides assessment and ways of intervention. There is a sense in which the counsellor has now developed their own individual style and is less dependent on a 'right way of counselling'. There is competency in a range of skills, an awareness of their strengths and limitations, and an ability to be autonomous with clients whilst realizing the need for ongoing supervision and training. Such a counsellor was the supervisee who returned to a supervisory session saying, 'Thank you for your help with the client last week: I thought a lot about your suggestion to work out a suicide contract with her, but I know it is not the right time and I would be putting her in a double-bind by doing that just now.'

If we accept that trainees move through training in a systematic way, then it seems important to gauge their client work according to their level. This helps in two ways. It means the trainee is not being put in an impossible situation by trying to do more than they are capable of, and it ensures that the needs of the client are being met by a trainee who is capable of working with them.

The level of client need

The level of client disturbance and the nature of their problems will give clues about how able trainees are to help. There are clients whose levels of disturbance, and whose ability to frighten and manipulate people are such that they need specialized help.

In a counselling agency in which I worked there was a 'groupie client', that is, one who moved from agency to agency getting counselling from as many people as possible. She was not really interested in changing but found the contact with the counsellor and the challenges involved exhilarating. Her strategy was, if at all possible, to get a beginning counsellor by presenting a fairly lightweight problem, and then proceeding to frighten her with alleged suicide attempts. Sometimes during a session she would disappear into the toilet for extended periods of time leaving the poor beginner to fantasize that she was cutting her wrists, having hinted beforehand that this is what she intended to do. She was adept at manipulation, at engendering fear in people. An experienced counsellor was eventually provided after two trainee counsellors were left frustrated, angry and de-skilled. Her level of disturbance required a counsellor with an understanding of how to work with such clients.

In agencies in which there are trainee counsellors I consider it best to have an experienced counsellor make an assessment and then determine the 'suitability' of the match between the beginner and the client. I disagree with the practice in settings such as GP surgeries where beginning counsellors see everyone sent by the doctor without any monitoring process. This seems to me to put an incredible burden on the trainee.

Client developmental issues (teenage problems, career, relationships) which tend to be of a transitory nature, are suitable for beginners. More deep set issues, for example, eating disorders, sexual abuse, depression, personality disorders, require more knowledge, different skills and often longer-term work. Trainees can be gradually introduced to this in a number of ways. Their training course can provide background information to psychological problem areas, for example, understanding depression and anxiety. There are a number of assessment procedures to help understand the signs and symptoms brought by clients. In addition, supervision can help to monitor and allay fears and anxieties as trainees find themselves out of their depth. Work with families and couples, as well as context-based work (for example, cross-cultural clients, counselling with residential clients) is specialized and would normally be reserved for the experienced practitioner.

Supervision as trainee monitor

Supervision is the prime area where trainees can evaluate their readiness to work with clients. This is the forum in which the trainee's skills and abilities are monitored and matched with the client's needs. A supervisor will know what is happening and will be able to advise about the match between counselling setting and trainee levels of skills and about which clients are best seen by trainees. I think Bernard and Goodyear's (1991: 2) definition of supervision brings out the concern for the welfare of the client and the introduction of the trainee to the profession of counselling:

> Supervision is a means of transmitting the skills, knowledge, and attitudes of a particular profession to the next generation in that

profession. It also is an essential means of ensuring that clients receive a certain minimum quality of care while trainees work with them to gain their skills.

Supervision is the forum which ensures that trainees are not pushed beyond their limitations, which easily results in their becoming de-skilled. Contact between the supervisor, the training course and the counselling setting or agency where the trainee is seeing clients, will add further support to the counsellor. The supervisor will be able to inform the agency when 'inappropriate' referrals are being made, and the training course can learn from both what training needs are not being met by the course.

Conclusion

As in all professions, trainee counsellors must start somewhere, and they learn primarily by engaging with clients in the art of counselling. That experience, in my estimation, needs to be monitored carefully so that the client is not harmed, and the trainee not demoralized. It is important that trainees develop and refine their skills and are gradually given the experience needed to progress to more complex counselling situations.

References and further reading

Bernard, J.M. and Goodyear, R.K. (1992) *Fundamentals of Clinical Supervision.* Boston: Allyn & Bacon.

Hawkins, P. and Shohet, R. (1989) *Supervision in the Helping Professions.* Milton Keynes: Open University Press.

Stoltenberg, C.D. and Delworth, U. (1987) *Supervising Counselors and Therapists: A Developmental Approach.* San Francisco: Jossey-Bass.

PART THREE

THE PERSONAL AND THE PRACTICAL

---

12   The counsellor's life crisis

What impact has going through a life crisis, such as the break-up of a marriage, had on the practice of your counselling?

Vanja Orlans

My marriage break-up, in the context of my broader journey, has generated numerous insights and issues which I have taken into my practice as a counsellor – some of these in a specific or more directly 'clinical' way, some as 'tips for living' which I can pass on to clients from my own experience, and some that are more global and generalized. In answering this question I would like to highlight both some general and specific learnings – reflections and thoughts about marriage and the breaking up of relationships which form 'the ground' for the emergence of particular 'figures' with special relevance to the clinical setting.

On being invited to write this piece I experienced a mixture of feelings ranging from excitement to anxiety. There were questions of what I would say and not say, ethical considerations concerning the divulging of personal information, the process of putting myself on the map in this way, and my recognition that in being open I would feel both more integrated and more vulnerable. Perhaps the established monogamous pattern of relationships, the standard domestic arrangement of marriage, had been so ingrained in my psyche as 'normal', thus evoking easily feelings of 'failure' in the face of publicizing the dissolution of such a structure. Yet even behind this lurked something else – it had to do with a sense almost of embarrassment – a part of me that found it difficult to articulate and own up publicly to the many *positive* learnings that have impacted on my practice as a counsellor and psychotherapist – as if this would somehow discount my pain and that of others.

For me it is also true that the process of 'dis-solving' – of facing some of the truths of my own and others' existence both prior to, and during, this experience – is proving to be one of the most challenging and growthful periods of my life. As I separate and reclaim my 'self', so I develop my capacity to make more creative and satisfying contact with those around me – friends and family as well as clients. At the same time it is an extremely painful and stressful experience, and one which has required much careful thought, non-idealistic choice, and commitment to personal learning – especially where there are children involved who can so easily become 'dumping grounds' for their parents' distress.

We live in a fragmented and structurally-oriented world which at one level is reflected in the 'stuck' places that clients (and prospective counsellors!) frequently inhabit when they first come to see a counsellor or psychotherapist. In the course of therapy we and our clients 'unfreeze' – we begin to move more freely between parts of ourselves, between polarities, and between parts of our existence in the world. The results of this process can be energizing and potentially more creative and satisfying than being trapped in the oppression of fixed structures – either within ourselves or in the wider world. And in the course of this process it is inevitable that certain 'shelters' will be challenged, and some may not be able to withstand the resulting turbulence. Several writers (for example, de Board, 1978; Merry and Brown, 1987, inter alia) have articulated the ways in which organizations and institutions are often creations of over-control and denial invested in the maintenance of the status quo and the reduction of negatively perceived anxiety or discomfort. Such places are vulnerable as people grow and develop and become less frightened, and it is important for counsellors to recognize such potential risks and challenges when clients come into counselling. Many counsellors will also share my own experience of clients who state at the outset that they wish to change, but that they do not want their major relationship to be affected!

The institution of marriage, as traditionally conceived, is an obvious structure to be challenged – particularly perhaps by a woman – as she grows and develops and empowers her Self. This does not mean that a marriage needs to end – this is only one of the options available – but it is likely that it will require some fundamental changes to meet evolving needs. The task of finding ways in which human beings can express their needs and capacities for intimacy within frameworks which allow for an imaginative mix of safety and creative exploration is a major challenge for all of us.

The break-up of my own marriage has been part of a broader and more profound 'existential project' in my life, and it would therefore be erroneous to attribute all my insights and learnings directly to this 'event'. At the same time, it will remain a poignant and significant marker of one of the most important transitions in my development as a person.

Below are some of the more specific insights which are relevant to my counselling practice. In their different ways, they are all concerned with changes in awareness and the resulting inevitable effects on the total 'field' which includes my functioning as a counsellor and psychotherapist, the way I run my practice and my relationship with my clients:

Empathy and related issues

At a global level, my experiences so far have enabled me to develop and sharpen my empathy in my work with clients. I now know from personal experience about the layers of relationship in a marriage, about the way in which loving does not simply stop, about the ambivalence inherent in this transition. Of course it is possible to be empathic without having been through this process, but I feel that I have acquired so many concrete examples of the complexities of untying cultural, legal, structural and emotional knots. As a consequence of this, I now appreciate much more fully the time it takes to 'unravel', and am thus in a better position to journey through this with a client. I now know that it takes years to leave a marriage, and I am consequently more patient and can pace my work more effectively with clients who are going through this process.

Confluence and countertransference

I am aware that those life experiences that potentially bring us closer to clients, and enable us better to understand their problems and challenges, can also potentially interfere in a negative way with the therapeutic process. There is the danger of being too close to the issue to have the independent perspective needed to be truly helpful – especially when, like me, the counsellor has not yet completed the separation process. There is always the risk, but especially so under conditions of severe environmental stress and personal vulnerability, that the counsellor's own unresolved issues can get in the way of clear contact with the client and can negatively affect the therapeutic process. My knowledge of this possibility has made me more vigilant – I have developed an internal 'red flashing light' whenever certain issues are presented – and has prompted me to depend more than usual on my supervision arrangements and support.

Existential dimensions

The break-up of my marriage, and the events which connect in various ways with this experience, have evoked in me a series of what I can only describe as existential crises – concerned with both fear and acceptance of death, isolation, loneliness, and the search for meaning in an uncertain world. From the point of view of my work with clients, particularly as a Gestalt counsellor and psychotherapist, these experiences have been invaluable as well as painful. My preparedness to experience events fully, and to have allowed myself at times to 'fall into the abyss' – that place of lostness, terror, helplessness and devastation – have provided me with a set of very useful resources for clients who wish to make such a journey themselves. The pain of these experiences has also sharpened my awareness of the difficulties involved in choosing either to stay in, or to leave, a marriage or relationship which is in important ways unsatisfying, and the usefulness of allowing clients plenty of space to explore this choice for themselves.

Taking responsibility and 'parenting'

My experiences have presented a profound challenge to my different internal states or 'selves', sometimes referred to as parent, adult and child ego states. At different times I have felt like an abandoned child, an over-controlling parent and an irresponsible adult. In working through these issues in my own therapy, as well as with my children and partner, I have been able to strengthen my 'grown-up' side, and have become a more competent parent both to my own inner child and to my other children. As a result, I feel much more confident in my skills and capacity to 're-parent' clients in the context of the reparative or developmentally needed relationship (Clarkson, 1990) in the course of the counselling process.

Cultural introjects and their effects

My experiences have made me particularly aware of the ways in which I have introjected so many of the traditional social and cultural norms surrounding coupledom, marriage and family life. This has reinforced my sense of the importance of distinguishing between 'a therapeutic issue' and 'a systems issue' in my work with clients – of particular importance in counselling approaches which can sometimes place unthinking emphasis on 'personal responsibility'. For example, the feelings of 'failure' which I have frequently experienced have turned out, very often, to be a *normal* response to a system of social control, rather than a therapeutic issue of my own.

Taking care of myself as a counsellor and psychotherapist

My marriage break-up has been (and continues to be) a significant death in my life. It has challenged me to find more useful and healthy ways of coping than simply 'struggling on' (a well known previous strategy of mine!). Grieving is an exhausting process and I have frequently felt tired and in need of much support. Over time I have learnt to keep clearer boundaries between work and leisure, I have on occasion cut down my work load considerably, I have called on the support of close friends and have made it a priority to maintain these important contacts, and have gained energy and support at different times from Chinese medicine, acupuncture, massage and cranial osteopathy. In the course of this, I have developed a wealth of useful tips for clients as well as proving to myself that only when I am prepared to take care of *me* can I authentically take care of others.

In reviewing the above points, I recognize the extent to which space has precluded doing full justice to the richness of some of my recent experiences and their relevance to my work. Crises and relationships are the stuff of counselling. Clients frequently arrive in the first place as a result of some major crisis and transition in their lives, often involving relationship changes in their world – a death of someone close, the transition into or out of marriage, loss of an intimate relationship, loss of a job, the birth of a child or the crisis of meaninglessness and isolation that comes from an awareness of the lack of intimacy in their lives. My own recent and ongoing experiences in this particular transition have, I believe, contributed significantly to my current and potential effectiveness as a counsellor. Perhaps the most important aspect has been my constant wish, and sometimes struggle, to view my experiences as opportunities for learning.

References

Clarkson, P. (1990) 'A multiplicity of psychotherapeutic relationships', *British Journal of Psychotherapy*, 7(2): 148–63.

de Board, R. (1978) *The Psychoanalysis of Organizations: A Psychoanalytic Approach to Behaviour in Groups and Organizations*. London: Tavistock Publications.

Merry, U. and Brown, G.I. (1987) *The Neurotic Behavior of Organizations*. New York: Gestalt Institute of Cleveland Press.

Editor's note

Interested readers might also like to consult *Beyond Transference: When the Therapist's Real Life Intrudes*, edited by J. Gold and J. Nemiah (American Psychiatric Press, Washington DC, 1993) for other examples of the effect of therapists' life crises on the therapeutic process.

13   When the counsellor shares the client's problem

Should a counsellor attempt to help someone with a problem when he or she has not resolved that problem in him/herself?

Elke Lambers

It is generally accepted in counselling that counsellors must not let their own problems get in the way of their work and that they have to withdraw from counselling if their functioning is impaired. This issue is addressed in the *Code of Ethics and Practice* of the British Association for Counselling (BAC, 1990: Paragraphs 2.2.18–19, 2.3.1).

Faced with a vast range of human experiences, counsellors will inevitably at times be reminded of their own past or current life experiences and their own vulnerability. What should counsellors do when in their work with clients they become aware of unresolved problems in themselves: perhaps one which they are encountering for the first time, or maybe an unexpected reminder of a difficulty which they thought had been left behind? Is it responsible, or even ethical, for them to work with this client?

This response will consider the extent to which the counsellor is able to be aware of such difficulties and present a checklist of questions which might be asked in supervision. Fictional examples will be given to illustrate various points.

Awareness

Unless counsellors are aware of the fact that they have met something which they have not resolved in themselves, they cannot ask themselves whether or not they should be working with a particular client. Sometimes this awareness is very immediate and clear, but more often counsellors will find themselves needing to focus on an initially vague awareness in order to develop a clear picture of their personal involvement. The following examples illustrate various complex ways in which the issue can present itself.

1   A client presents himself in the first session with a specific problem which the counsellor immediately recognizes as one which is particularly alive to her at the moment.

Example: The client is under stress due to difficulties in his marriage. The counsellor's relationship with her own partner is going through a difficult time.

2   As the client opens up more in the course of counselling she begins to talk about an issue which the counsellor realizes she (the counsellor) has not resolved herself.

Example: In session eight the client talks movingly about her feelings of loss which she still feels in relation to an abortion years ago. The counsellor is acutely reminded of her own sense of loss through not being able to have a child herself. She worked on this in her own therapy and is taken aback by the strong bitterness and anger she suddenly feels.

3   The client's way of dealing with her problem puts the counsellor in touch with painful memories or feelings.

Example: In the process of 'becoming herself' the client experiments with new ways of being which seem self-centred and hurtful to others. She is angry at the reactions of relatives and friends. This brings back feelings for the counsellor: she and her parents went through a terrible time when her sister joined a cult movement. She has never been able to really forgive her sister for this.

4   The counsellor's problem is meshing with the client's needs.

Example: The client wants to work through her experience of sexual abuse. She is lonely, scared of intimacy and has been hurt in a series of relationships where she was very dependent. The male counsellor has difficulties with intimacy, but is only partially aware of this. He loves his counselling work, particularly with long-term clients. He feels immediately that he can offer this client something – they seem to have 'clicked' very quickly.

The more fundamentally a problem is linked with the counsellor's personality, the less likely it is that he or she will be fully aware of what is being touched and of the potential effect of this on his or her work with the client.

The counsellor in Example 1 probably has a better chance of

recognizing what is going on than her colleague in Example 4 who may never recognize the difficulty on his own.

In Examples 3 and 4 the counsellors are aware of strong feelings, but they may not have recognized that they have discovered something unresolved in themselves.

Supervision is clearly essential for all the counsellors in the above examples. Counsellors who are confronted with something of emotional importance to themselves cannot necessarily trust themselves completely in their reflection on their work and in the decisions they make. Within the supportive and challenging context of supervision they can be helped to focus on issues which are on the edge of their awareness, issues which they are perhaps scared to face. They can step back from their work and create space to reflect on the best course of action, both for the client and for themselves.

To work or not to work?

With the help of supervision the counsellor can now begin to explore the question which is fundamental in this situation: 'Will I be able to detach myself sufficiently from my own problem and the feelings attached to it, to be fully present for the client?' The following 'checklist' may help counsellors focus on different aspects of their work with clients:

1 Will I be able to listen with empathy, hearing the client's experience rather than identifying with him or her or projecting my own feelings on to him or her?
2 Will I be able to listen to the client's distress without needing to protect myself from it?
3 Will I be able to allow the client to express him or herself freely, helping him or her to find his or her own direction rather than taking responsibility for him or her, protecting or rescuing him or her, or taking his or her side?
4 Will I be able to accept him or her rather than become conditional in my acceptance and judge, criticize or reject him or her?
5 Will I be able to get close to the client, or will I remain distant through being protective of myself, or through being too involved in monitoring myself?
6 Will I be able to be therapeutically congruent, able to distinguish between feelings which belong to the client and feelings which belong to me?

If the answer to any one of these questions is a definite 'No', then

I would suggest that the counsellor's functioning is impaired, and that he or she should seriously consider discontinuing his or her work with the client.

In the process of making such a major decision some other questions also need to be explored, for example:

1 What would it mean to the client if we stopped working together at this point in the therapeutic process?
2 How can I best address the issue with the client?
3 Can I refer the client to someone else? How can I do this sensitively?
4 What help do I need?
5 Can this situation happen again? Should I be doing more personal development work?

Much more common is the situation where the counsellor cannot give a definite 'Yes' or 'No' in answer to any of the six fundamental questions and where, for a variety of reasons, it is considered better to continue working with the client. In that case the counsellor will need to monitor his or her work very carefully and he or she will need to consider what support they need to help them to continue. Extra supervision sessions are almost certainly required and it may be necessary to enter into personal therapy or engage in some other form of relevant personal development work.

In Example 2 introduced earlier the counsellor continued with the client:

> The counsellor realized that in her own therapy she had not fully recognized her anger and bitterness about her childlessness. After talking it through with her supervisor she decided to arrange personal therapy. As far as her work with the client was concerned she discovered that the anger was her own and that she was not angry with the client. She felt that they had come a long way together, and she did not want her own feelings to get in the way. She identified empathic listening and congruent self-awareness as areas to focus on for the moment. This would help her to 'get back to the client' again.

Positive effects

Although I have focused so far on the possible negative effects of facing a problem similar to that of the client, I believe that sometimes the therapeutic relationship may benefit, provided that counsellors can use their own experience congruently, creatively and with the interest of the client the paramount concern.

Counsellors' extra effort to be fully present may result in greater intimacy and depth in the therapeutic relationship. Clients may experience counsellors' willingness to be open and to share some of their own experiences (without inappropriate self-disclosure) as respecting and trusting, which in turn might enhance the therapeutic quality of the relationship.

Counsellor's work on self

As counsellors it is our responsibility to seek opportunities for self-development and personal growth through personal therapy, supervision, training and other forms of personal development work. Simply to recognize and accept our own vulnerability and our limitations is not enough, we need to develop ourselves in all aspects of our functioning: personal and professional, cognitive and affective, so that we can be more and more fully available to our clients.

However, we also need to accept that we cannot be perfect, that we cannot always trust ourselves completely and that we may have blind spots.

As counsellors we are in a powerful position in relation to our clients; lack of awareness of ourselves and our own responses can lead to abuse of that power. But counsellors who think they know what they are doing can be as abusive of their clients as those who are not aware of their own process.

Reference

BAC (1990) *Code of Ethics and Practice for Counsellors*. Rugby: British Association for Counselling.

14 Spirituality and the counsellor

I am an atheist and find the whole area of spirituality in counselling confusing. My problem lies in the vague, wishy-washy ways in which people discuss this topic. I want to understand it better, so can you give me a brief description of spirituality in counselling and its value for a confused atheist?

Brian Thorne

I am not surprised that you find the area of spirituality confusing and I can imagine that, as an atheist, you must be somewhat daunted by the recent upsurge of interest in this area throughout the whole counselling world. Perhaps it is important therefore at the outset to separate the notion of spirituality from a belief structure which posits the existence of God or an elaborated system of religious dogma. As far as the counsellor is concerned, spirituality has relevance primarily because it concerns the nature of the self and the relationship between counsellor and client.

There have been many attempts to formulate theories of the self ranging from complex maps of the unconscious to a view of human nature based on biological drives or behaviourally conditioned reflexes. Every counsellor will have his or her own working concept of the self whether this is fully conscious and articulated or not. For the counsellor or client who takes the spiritual dimension seriously, however, this concept of the self, whether it incorporates, for example, the power of the unconscious, the need for unconditional love or even the influence of intra-uterine experience, will affirm that the ultimate foundation of our being is spiritual and that it is in the spiritual dimension that the true source of who we are is to be found.

The implications of this view of human nature are profound. Sadly, however, as John Rowan amongst others has shown (Rowan, 1990) one of the great problems around spirituality is that it is highly resistant to language. This may well be why you find yourself complaining about the 'vague, wishy-washy ways' in which the subject is often discussed. The reason for this resistance to language lies in the fact that spirituality goes beyond psychology and beyond any discipline which relies principally on language for its expression and is limited to it. Nonetheless if I hold to a concept of the self (as I do) which affirms spirit to be the fundamental ingredient, then it is incumbent upon me to do battle with language however resistant. For me the individual's spirit or spiritual dimension is his or her creative source of energy which reflects the moving force within the universe itself. In other words, it is because I am essentially a spiritual being that I am, whether I know it or not or whether I like it or not, indissolubly linked to all that is or has been or will be. I am not an isolated entity but rather a unique part of the whole created order. What is more this spiritual essence of my being defines me in a way which goes far beyond my genetic inheritance, my conditioning and all the ramifications of my unconscious processes. Furthermore, although at the present time my spiritual being manifests itself in the material form of my corporeal existence, it is not limited to that form. As Jill Hall has succinctly expressed it, 'Matter cannot be without spirit and is thus indivisible from spirit, although spirit can be without matter' (Hall, 1990). Spirit itself, unlike matter, is not subject to destruction which means that my fundamental self transcends the boundaries of time and space.

It may be that this attempt on my part to find language to express the spiritual nature of the self has left you more confused than ever. Let me come at the subject from a different angle. I would suggest that from time to time most of us are struck by extraordinary coincidences or we have sudden premonitions or we may be overwhelmed by powerful feelings of love or of oneness. If we are less fortunate, we get caught up in fearful anxieties or we sense the appalling power of evil or we are unaccountably plunged into the most unimaginable despair. At the time such experiences feel very real and they may affect us profoundly but frequently we fail to integrate them into our concept of reality and we do not see their relevance to an understanding of our own natures. They are likely to remain as 'coincidences' or 'feelings which came over me' or 'peak experiences' or 'waking nightmares'. We are less likely to say to ourselves that we have entered a world infinitely more extensive and astonishing than the work-a-day reality to which we are normally confined. In short, we may fail to acknowledge that, because we are spiritual beings, we have access to levels of experiencing which transcend by far the narrow boundaries of our rational world.

How on earth could all this be of use to you, as an atheist, in your work as a counsellor? In the first place, it might encourage you to entertain a different concept of your own nature and that of your client. Second, it might help you to accompany more effectively those clients for whom their spirituality is a basic assumption. Most importantly, however, it might make you less anxious as a counsellor and enable you to tap into resources which at the moment are perhaps denied you because you cannot credit their existence. Let me explain this last remark by reference to my own experience. For me, apart from certain fundamental and transforming experiences which I had as a young boy, my confrontation with the spiritual dimension of my own being has come about principally through the exercise of my profession as a counsellor. Frequently – and increasingly in recent years – both in individual and group counselling, I have been privileged to experience what I call 'magic moments'. Often such moments are the signal for a particular intensity of relating in which a new level of understanding is achieved and a powerful sense of validation by both client and counsellor. Outwardly situations may remain unchanged and the client's predicament, for example, may seem as intractable as ever. And yet, everything is different because a new creative energy has been tapped into which could variously be described as the power of love, the spirit of hope or the sense of ultimate security. Sometimes such 'magic moments' lead to an acceptance of powerlessness on my part, an acceptance which is not a sign of resignation, a kind of 'I give up' syndrome but rather something which unites counsellor and client and leads to a waiting without expectation but also without despair.

I believe that such acceptance of powerlessness is rare in our culture. We tend to want solutions and to expect an answer to every problem (often to be provided by an expert). We become frustrated and angry when no solution seems to be available. The acceptance of powerlessness of which I speak, however, is a recognition of our own limitations and at the same time an acknowledgement of the infinite resources by which we are surrounded. In such a context I find as the counsellor that I am no longer anxious to prove myself to be the 'good' therapist who has to provide all the right answers or facilitate all the right developments. What is more the client, too, can relax into not knowing without being frightened or frustrated. I have come to regard this acceptance of powerlessness as one of the major fruits of trusting in the spiritual foundation of the created order and of human nature. It leads to a waiting upon the spirit which is almost always creative and which frequently leads to unexpected outcomes. Such waiting seems to transcend normal time boundaries and has the powerful effect of removing anxiety about the future. In short, counsellor and client experience their place in the spiritual order and live, even if only briefly, in the light of eternity. At such moments living in the present becomes not only desirable but easy.

A final challenge if you are by now almost persuaded that I am not completely off my head. When you are next stuck in your work with a client, acknowledge your stuckness and invite your client to join you in waiting without anxiety for the process to unfold. If you genuinely care for your client and if he or she knows that you care, you may well be astonished by what follows. You will also know something about what many of your colleagues call spirituality even if you choose never to employ the word.

References

Hall, J. (1990) 'Transformation in counselling', *British Journal of Guidance and Counselling*, 18(3): 269–80.

Rowan, J. (1990) 'Spiritual experiences in counselling', *British Journal of Guidance and Counselling*, 18(3): 233–49.

15 When values clash

Can counsellors effectively work with clients whose values they find abhorrent?

Moira Walker

At the end of a long week, having assessed many new clients in a setting where we never know who will present, or with what difficulties; and having accepted most (apart from those where counselling is not appropriate), I find myself perplexed and more than a little irritated by this question. My mind turns initially to practicalities, and this leads me to first explore some pragmatic ramifications of the possibility of answering with a simple 'No'. How am I to discover the values of my potential client? Do I at the assessment stage also explore the value system of my possible new client in addition to my normal procedures? If I do so and I then discover their values are 'abhorrent' to me, what am I to do? Reject them? Send them away? Tell them I cannot work with them because I do not like what they believe? And what if this new client also happens to be extremely distressed? Perhaps we have to decide on what basis a client is to be accepted for counselling; is it that they are distressed, in need and able to work in that mode, or is it that the counsellor likes the person presenting? Given that many counsellors fall into the middle-class liberal bracket, with concomitant value systems, the potential client group could become even more restricted than it already is in terms of class, culture and age of client. Surely counselling should be exploring ways of increasing its accessibility to other sections of the community, rather than decreasing its range still further?

I am also aware that the values of any client may only gradually unfold as the process continues. After three months of counselling, it transpired that the gentle young man I was working with, who was depressed and lacking in self-esteem, and towards whom I had felt comfortably empathetic, was actually a member of the National Front. He held rabidly fascist and sexist views. Personally, I found (and find) those views and the philosophy of life they encompass deeply unacceptable and personally quite distressing. However, my contract with him did not have an exclusion clause allowing me to withdraw if I found I did not like his views. I had to continue working with him, and I had to work effectively. I could not simply dismiss him. I cannot be value free, and I have no desire to turn myself into a politically and therapeutically neutral blank screen. I have to own and acknowledge my own values, work on and with my own counter-transference, and in this instance I had to accept my dislike of my client's different and opposing views. However, I still have a professional responsibility to ensure that I work with the material that is presented to me.

The reader may ask if this is really possible, or if it is simply human nature that any counsellor works more effectively with clients with whom they feel psychologically and politically in tune? It could be perceived and understood as a reality that is unavoidable and therefore has to be accepted as such. However, the example of the young man illustrates how this need not be the case. In the session where this new information was revealed I certainly sensed a strong antipathy towards him. I did nothing with that feeling; for me it is a valuable rule of thumb that if in doubt I keep quiet, and go away and think about it. I discussed the situation with colleagues and my supervisor. I left them in no doubt as to my own feelings on these matters; in fact I expressed them volubly and at some length.

This was a valuable release for my feelings, it made me feel temporarily better, but it was not sufficient. I was still left with the client and I had to see him again in our next session. I then started thinking and considering how I could work with this material. I wondered what it meant in terms of our relationship and why he had told me at this point. I wondered what membership of this group meant to him and what need it was meeting. I reminded myself that he was a very unhappy young man, who often felt suicidal and who was desperately searching for something to validate him. I remembered that in early sessions he told me how he sabotaged all his relationships when they threatened to become too close and how he could 'turn nasty' with women. It began to seem that the latter was actually being played out with me; after all, it would not be too difficult for my client to recognize that I would not be sympathetic to his views.

It felt that he was both attempting to sabotage and be nasty. I was able to begin to explore these issues with him, in the course of which I acknowledged that I did not agree with his views, pointing out that it was not for me to impose alternatives on him – that was his choice – but we could together attempt to understand why he had made these choices and what they meant to him. Approaching the material in this way proved a watershed in my work with this client. A negative transference developed, and in working with and through this, his rigid and somewhat extreme views started to change. As time went by his depression started to lift; his suicidal feelings disappeared and the quality of his relationships improved. He left the National Front, and joined the Conservative Party, explaining this as a sensible career move. I still intensely disliked his values. He remained sexist and racist, although in a less extreme way. I imagine his conservative views were similar to those held dear by a large proportion of the population. I do not agree with them. I suspect he similarly continued to disagree with mine. However, in the end I think we quite liked one another, although in this description the reader may find it hard to imagine why. I think we had become sparring partners who could respect each other's differences.

This is an example of an effective piece of work with a client whose values were in many essential ways anathema to me. It was not easy; and he was not a client I would have chosen for myself had that choice existed. However, most of those who choose to work in the caring professions cannot indulge themselves in the luxury of picking and choosing their client or patient group. This is true of social workers, doctors, nurses and psychologists. The question needs to be asked whether counselling and therapy should be any different? If it is really felt that counsellors cannot work effectively with clients whose values they find abhorrent (a very strong word to use) then counselling is in grave danger of appearing ridiculously self-indulgent and overly precious. If counselling is to be seen as a service for those in psychological distress, then it has to operate as such. It cannot cocoon itself against a world that contains much that many of us dislike.

It is easy to assume that whereas it can be effective, if inevitably a struggle, to work with clients who hold values that are problematic to the counsellor, working with clients who hold similar views and values will be more straightforward. It may in some respects be more comfortable and harmonious to work with those who understand the world from our point of view but this does not mean that the process is without its own struggles, although they are of a different nature. There is a danger in this situation of becoming cosy and collusive, and of appropriate challenges and interventions being left unmade. It need not be so; but the point I am making is that struggling with difficulties of one sort or another is frequently an intrinsic part of the therapeutic process, although it takes different forms in different situations and dilemmas.

If I were to answer this question in one line I would give my daughter's response when she was watching me write: 'Of course you have to, it's your job. You can't tell people to go away if they're unhappy, just because you don't agree with them.' Perhaps that is the bottom line. Perhaps there is a grave danger of counselling becoming overly selective and narrow, and becoming too concerned with the angst of the counsellor and losing the agony of the client. I think that there are occasions when counsellors should avoid working with certain situations for their own and their clients' protection. If counsellors have unresolved personal issues of their own, it is obviously advisable that they avoid the same situations with clients until their own have been sufficiently resolved (see Chapter 13). For example, a woman counsellor who has herself been a rape victim can ultimately work very well with others in that situation. However, she can only do so when her own feelings have settled enough for her not to project her own experiences on to others, and when her own pain has become tolerable. Counsellors who work with others in a team can sensibly and helpfully use their resources by acknowledging and using their different skills. In this sense some choice of clients is then helpful and appropriate. But this is a very different scenario from one that states that effective work can only be undertaken if the values of the counsellor and client are sufficiently similar. Whilst that may seem an appealing scenario it is not one that accurately reflects the real world and if counselling is to be taken seriously it needs to place itself firmly within that world, rather than simply creating one of its own.

PART FOUR

BEYOND SPECIFIC ORIENTATIONS

16 Choosing an eclectic, not syncretic, psychotherapist

*I am a trainee counsellor seeking personal therapy.
I don't want to see a therapist who is tied to a
single therapeutic approach, preferring to work
with someone who is integrative in their work. But
how do I know whether a counsellor who
describes him- or herself as eclectic or integrative is
disciplined in integration or muddle-headed?*

John C. Norcross and Thomas J. Tomcho

Mental health professionals regularly cite personal therapy as a vital contributor to their professional development, and many consider it a desirable, if not necessary, prerequisite for clinical work. Fully 96 per cent of British clinical psychologists who underwent personal therapy, for instance, found it to be valuable preparation for their counselling activities (Norcross, Dryden and DeMichele, 1992). Accordingly, we are pleased that a trainee counsellor is voluntarily seeking personal therapy as one component of his or her education.

We are doubly pleased that you are carefully considering both the theoretical orientation and the professional competence in that orientation of your prospective psychotherapist. Although eclecticism is the most popular theoretical orientation among mental health professionals, most counsellors acquire their eclectic stance idiosyncratically and perhaps serendipitously. Training counsellors to competence in multiple theories and interventions is unprecedented in the comparatively brief history of psychotherapy; that is, most contemporary clinicians have drifted toward eclecticism on their own, without formal training.

As a result, some self-designated 'eclectic' or 'integrative' counsellors are, in actuality, practising *syncretism*: an arbitrary and unsystematic blending of concepts from two or more of the 400 plus 'schools' of psychotherapy (Lazarus, Beutler and Norcross, 1992). Their pluralistic intentions are to be commended, but their haphazard hybrids are an outgrowth of pet techniques and inadequate training. Dryden (1986) observes that many of these counsellors wander around in a daze of professional nihilism, experimenting with new 'fads' indiscriminately. Eysenck (1970: 145) characterizes this indiscriminate smørgasbord as a 'mish-mash of theories, a hugger-mugger of procedures, a gallimaufry of therapies', having no proper rationale or empirical verification. This muddle of idiosyncratic and ineffable clinical creations is the antithesis of effective and efficient psychotherapy (Lazarus, Beutler and Norcross, 1992).

Systematic eclecticism, by contrast, is the product of years of painstaking clinical research and experience. It is truly eclecticism 'by design', that is, clinicians competent in several therapeutic systems who prescriptively apply or withhold interventions based on patient need and comparative outcome research. Only a systematic form of eclecticism can be taught, replicated and evaluated. All systematic thinking involves the synthesis of pre-existing points of views. It is not a question of whether or not to be eclectic but of whether or not to be disciplined and systematic.

Think of this distinction between eclecticism (by design) and syncretism (by default) as the process of quilt making. Quilt makers do not mechanically select their swatches from the entire universe of cloth. Instead, the possible materials are restricted to those in their possession, to remnants of old projects, and to those that can be readily acquired (in psychological terms: psychoanalytic, behavioural, experiential, etc.). One cannot include materials that one does not possess. Furthermore, one can construct a quilt out of incomplete materials and scraps (by default) or, alternatively, from an abundance of rich and diverse materials (by design). Because they must peddle their wares in the public marketplace, the more effective quilt makers customize their products to match consumer's needs, not their own desires. We would obviously prefer, be it in purchasing quilts or psychotherapy, to partake of the services of a talented artisan acting on the needs of the client and from an abundance of competencies.

How, then, would one proceed in selecting a systematic eclectic rather than a syncretist for one's personal therapy? Five guidelines come to mind, guidelines that probably apply with equal cogency to competence in any clinical activity but are all the more urgent in a nascent field such as psychotherapy integration.

1 *Extent of formal training and supervised experience in eclecticism.* As you interview a few prospective therapists, you could ask: Where was your training in eclecticism? Who were your instructors? Beyond your training in specific methods and particular counselling systems, where did you learn to put them all together? How much formal supervision did you receive in eclecticism? Answers to questions such as these should begin to demarcate between the 'weekend warriors' who are defaulting toward syncretism and extensively trained eclectics who are customizing psychological treatment to individual clients.

2 *Ability to articulate a systematic model of eclecticism.* You might ask your prospective therapist the following questions: Which theoretical systems do you blend? On what *basis* do you select the techniques to employ in a given case? Can you describe how your work differs from a muddle-headed 'seat of the pants' approach? How do you operationalize the decision-making process regarding such choice-points as the indicated therapy formats (individual, family, group), therapeutic alliance and stage of treatment (Dryden, 1986)? A response or, better yet, a published article or conference presentation containing a coherent rationale or scheme by which to choose technical interventions and relationship stance augurs well for a disciplined approach.

3 *Familiarity with the burgeoning eclectic literature.* Directly ask the potential therapist: Do you subscribe to integrative periodicals (for example, *Journal of Psychotherapy Integration*), belong to relevant organizations (for example, Society for the Exploration of Psychotherapy Integration), own seminal books and recent handbooks (for example, Norcross and Goldfried, 1992) on the topic? Responses to these queries may begin to distinguish between counsellors vaguely aligning themselves with pluralistic notions and counsellors embracing an eclectic model as a guide for more comprehensive and empirically-driven practice.

4 *Receipt of standard credentials and professional recognition.* Representative questions here would include: Are you accredited by the British Association for Counselling, or chartered as a psychologist, or a member of one of the organizations recognized by the United Kingdom Council for Psychotherapy? Have you gathered data on your client outcomes? Have you been recommended by or formally recognized by an organization devoted to psychotherapy integration? Although psychotherapy integration is too young a movement to have established widely-accepted credentials,

advocates of systematic eclecticism should have achieved some certification or membership in their respective professions and should have attempted to collect empirical data on their success rates. After all, the ultimate objective of psychotherapy integration is to enhance treatment outcome.

5 *Capacity for disciplined innovation and improvisation.* Ask such questions as: How do you decide when to alter your initial treatment plan? Could you give me a recent clinical example in which you tried something innovative with a client? A thoughtful and reflective manner of responding to these and related questions speaks well of a prospective therapist; try to listen not only to the content of the clinical improvisation but also to the reasoning process behind such decisions.

A systematic eclectic, as we have already stated, should be able to articulate explicit decision-making criteria and a coherent rationale for treatment planning. This ability parallels the dictionary definition of *eclecticism* – 'selecting what appears to be best in various doctrines, methods, or styles'. Professionals need to exercise responsible discretion in matching techniques to unique clients and individual problems.

While the primary basis for the prescriptive matching will be research knowledge, psychotherapy will remain what Schacht (1991) calls 'disciplined innovation'. Like a jazz pianist, the counsellor must acquire factual knowledge, master technical skills and appreciate artistic principles. Then – and only then – the disciplined innovator must combine these elements in unique, innovative and yet coherently integrated performances. By word and deed, does your potential counsellor behave in a creatively synthetic fashion (as opposed to a mindless 'seat of the pants' manner) in clinical work? Is she or he able to balance the need for a coherent treatment plan with the need for disciplined flexibility in responding to the differing needs of one person to another, one occasion to another?

Finally, as committed as we are to the advancement of psychotherapy integration, we would heartily advise you – and others in similar circumstances – to consider more than theoretical orientation in choosing a counsellor. Available research indicates that the principal reasons for therapist selection and the active ingredients of effective counselling resides outside specific theories and techniques. Therapists choose their own therapists largely on the grounds of competence, clinical experience, professional reputation, warmth and caring (theoretical orientation ranked sixth in importance on a list of sixteen possible selection criteria

(Norcross, Strausser and Faltus, 1988)); the lasting lessons accrued from the experience of personal therapy largely concern the centrality of a facilitative therapeutic relationship and nurturing interpersonal skills (Norcross, Dryden and DeMichele, 1992).

So, yes, by all means choose a systematic eclectic over a muddle-headed syncretist for your personal therapist but also select one possessing relevant experience, a stellar reputation, interpersonal warmth and genuine caring for the person you are and for the counsellor you are becoming.

References

Dryden, W. (1986) 'Eclectic psychotherapies: a critique of leading approaches', in J.C. Norcross (ed.), *Handbook of Eclectic Psychotherapy*. New York: Brunner/Mazel.

Eysenck, H.J. (1970) 'A mish-mash of theories', *International Journal of Psychiatry*, 9: 140–6.

Lazarus, A.A., Beutler, L.E. and Norcross, J.C. (1992) 'The future of technical eclecticism', *Psychotherapy*, 29: 11–20.

Norcross, J.C., Dryden, W. and DeMichele, J.T. (1992) 'British clinical psychologists and personal therapy: what's good for the goose?' *Clinical Psychology Forum*, 44: 29–33.

Norcross, J.C. and Goldfried, M.R. (eds) (1992) *Handbook of Psychotherapy Integration*. New York: Basic Books.

Norcross, J.C., Strausser, D.J. and Faltus, F.J. (1988) 'The therapist's therapist', *American Journal of Psychotherapy*, 42: 53–66.

Schacht, T.E. (1991) 'Can psychotherapy education advance psychotherapy integration?' *Journal of Psychotherapy Integration*, 1: 305–19.

17 Reservations about eclectic and integrative approaches to counselling

I understand that you have strong reservations about eclectic and integrative approaches to counselling. What are they?

Sue Wheeler

In order to answer your question I need to clarify what I understand the critical terms used in it, namely 'eclectic' and 'integrative', to mean. An eclectic approach to counselling conveys to me a counsellor's ability to draw from a range of skills and expertise in different therapy modes, according to the needs and circumstances of the client or setting. An integrative approach to counselling implies that one or more established models of therapy or counselling are welded together, to produce a hybrid. The model may be unique to the individual counsellor, according to their own mix, or may be one of the models for which supportive literature exists, such as Egan's Three-stage Model, Cognitive Behavioural Therapy or Cognitive Analytic Therapy.

Let me first comment on eclecticism. I have no reservations about counsellors who have had a sound professional training in two or more models of counselling, choosing to use their competence in one model or another according to circumstances. As for counsellors using an integrative model, I have no reservations as long as the model is one that has a sound theoretical and skills base that they have been rigorously trained to use.

However, my knowledge and experience of counsellor training in Britain informs me that there are few courses which prepare counsellors to be either professionally eclectic or integrative as described above, although many counselling courses in Britain describe themselves as eclectic. Using my definition of a professional eclectic, the courses would need to be at least five or six years long, part time, in order for the criteria of professional competence in two or more models to be achieved. In practice courses are rarely more than two years or 450 hours in duration, and may cover a range of diverse models in that time.

Common practice is for an 'eclectic' course to organize short modules on different counselling models, offering selected highlights from the theory and practical skills intrinsic to them. Arnold Lazarus (1981) has researched and developed an integrative eclectic approach called 'Multimodal therapy' but although this may be referred to on eclectic courses, I know of no course that adheres to Multimodal therapy as its core model. Students on eclectic courses risk becoming 'a jack of all trades and master of none'. They tend to have a flimsy grasp of a range of theories, each with a different ideological base, that are unintegrated and probably unintegratable! If there is no core theoretical model that is studied in depth, students have no secure frame of reference in which to conceptualize their clients' concerns or on which to rely when the going gets tough. Such an 'eclectic' course does not provide a professional training that enables the counsellor to choose from a range of approaches in which they are proficient, but leaves them dabbling with oversimplified techniques.

Some courses describe themselves as integrative, but this claim does not always bear close examination. To some extent, all counselling training is integrative, as models of counselling have evolved from psychotherapy, psychoanalysis, social learning theory, developmental psychology and interpersonal skills. Many counselling models that we are working with today have been documented and debated, and give us literature to refer to and a reference point from which to grow and develop. There are also reputable integrative models that can be studied in depth. However, many courses either cultivate their own integrative model, by offering bits of this and bits of that without always explaining exactly how it all fits together, or expect their students to mix and match and integrate their own brand of therapy. I do not wish to stifle creativity, and indeed seek to encourage new ideas but it seems to me that integration is a highly complex process, involving the consideration of many factors, and it is too much to expect novice counsellors to undertake such a task. I also question how students' knowledge and skill in an ad hoc integrative counselling model can be evaluated, when guidelines are fluid.

I will stick my neck out even further by venturing another criticism of eclectic or integrative courses, which is that sometimes tutors themselves are only capable of offering watered down highlights of different models, because that is all that they have experienced in their own training. Inevitably, as so many courses in Britain are eclectic, unless individuals have chosen to take further training in a particular theoretical model, the knowledge of trainers will become diluted. Some courses would defend this challenge by inviting 'experts' who work with different theoretical models, to lead sessions. However, I wonder how often the 'experts' meet with the principal trainers to thrash out the way in which their theory can be successfully integrated with other approaches, or how often the inexperienced trainees are left to work it out for themselves.

There is a small but increasing amount of research into the effectiveness of counselling, and the differential effectiveness of models. The time is fast approaching in the United States when counsellors may be sued for malpractice if they do not use the most effective counselling treatment model for the problem presented. Perhaps it is important for counsellors to have a range of skills, but they must be fully competent to use that range. The amount of training that is sufficient to achieve competence is a subject for debate.

I argue that a solid training in one core theoretical model, whatever that may be, gives a trainee counsellor a coherent framework to work with, from which they can venture out and explore other theories, which they may eventually integrate, or in which they may choose to retrain at a later date, to become a 'true' eclectic. Fritz Perls, Carl Jung, Eric Berne and many other theoreticians started with an analytic training, from which they evolved and developed their own ideas.

In order to produce an integrative or eclectic course of study that is both rigorous and cohesive, attention needs to be focused on a range of issues, including the following. First, what assumptions are made about the psychological development of human beings and how is the development and maintenance of psychological problems accounted for? The theories postulated by different models range from people being inherently good and self-actualizing, to their being inherently bad, with a constant need to suppress murderous and self-destructive instincts. Psychological problems may be attributed to the environment, family, life experiences, or to unconscious processes and internalized objects. It seems to me that an intuitive decision has to be made about the power and influence of the unconscious and the treatment model must reflect that understanding. Rogerian and psychoanalytic perspectives do not hang together well in this domain!

Second, what is understood to be the nature of therapeutic change, the nature of the therapeutic relationship and the range of interventions that facilitate change? In different models change is understood to be achieved by insight into unconscious processes, catharsis or self-acceptance. Therapeutic relationships may require the counsellor to be warm, accepting and genuine, opaque, unemotional and thoughtful, or active, directive and challenging. Some models acknowledge the existence of transference and see it as an essential aspect of the relationship, and others ignore or deny it. Interventions may be directive and structured, they may be based on an emotional response to the client, or may be interpretations of unconscious material. The whole is more than a sum of the parts, and it is a challenge to be able to make sense of and use all these perspectives.

To summarize, my strong reservations about eclectic and integrative approaches to counselling are to do with training rather than these approaches per se. I have no objections to a counsellor being well qualified to work with say, Transactional Analysis or Behaviour Therapy, and choosing one or other mode with specific clients as appropriate. I have personal reservations about some integrative models, but in general do not object to counsellors using a well described and researched integrative model in which they have had substantial training. My strong feelings are about idiosyncratic eclecticism that encourages counsellors to incorporate various ideas and methods on the basis of subjective appeal, and about training courses that do not provide a sound theoretical integrative framework that can be used to underpin and give meaning to clinical encounters.

Reference

Lazarus, A.A. (1981) *The Practice of Multimodal Therapy*. New York: McGraw-Hill.

18 Beyond Egan

I understand that you have completed a training in Psychosynthesis. You are still well known for being a proponent of 'the skilled helper' model of Gerard Egan. What do you consider Psychosynthesis has added to your practice that the Egan model failed to offer?

Francesca Inskipp

To answer this question I need to outline briefly how I developed my original theory and philosophy of counselling. I will then describe how Egan has influenced my work and finally how my 3-year Diploma in Psychosynthesis with the Psychosynthesis and Education Trust has changed my work – and my life.

I trained originally at the University of Keele in 1970/1 on a Diploma Course designed to train counsellors to work in schools and colleges – I took the college option. The course was one of the two early Diplomas set up with the help of American colleagues and used books written by American counsellors. The course emphasis was much derived from Vocational Guidance and Developmental Counselling but the work of Carl Rogers was the primary influence. We also had a visiting American professor who was behaviourally oriented and did quite a bit of the teaching. My practical work was taught and supervised by the Keele counsellors who included Audrey Newsome and Brian Thorne, both client-centred practitioners. Coming to the course as a rather bossy, directive teacher these influences changed my whole way of seeing and being; it was a big emotional upheaval and reading Rogers (1975) *On Becoming a Person* still moves me. However, I've always been driven by time – the efficient use of time – and the large number of sessions often used by Rogers when he worked with clients, did not seem to equate with the resources available to work with college students, as I saw it, though his core qualities of empathy, unconditional positive regard and congruence became my guiding light in counselling and teaching. I found Behavioural Counselling and Rational-Emotive Therapy tied in with my desire to take short cuts and to move clients on; but this seemed to give me a lot of power to direct clients, when my philosophy was urging me to empower my clients to find their own ways of being.

Towards the end of the course, Robert Carkhuff came to spend several days with us and expounded his model (Carkhuff, 1969), in which the core qualities were necessary and essential but not sufficient. He added four additional skills which he designated 'the action-oriented skills': concreteness, self-disclosure, confrontation and immediacy in the relationship. This made sense to me and suited my action-oriented personality but allowed me to keep the valued core qualities. As a last gift from Keele I received a draft book *The Counsellor in Training* written by Susan Gilmore (1973) a student of Leonie Tyler who was one of the 'godmothers' of the Keele course. The book focused on ways of developing the core qualities – how to become more empathic, more accepting, more congruent and how to teach and learn the skills of communicating these qualities. I also did some research on micro-skills training and enjoyed Ivey's work on training para-professionals. I returned to my job as a trainer in Youth and Community Service with a lot of ideas on training which I was able to try out by designing and running short courses for a variety of professional workers; I also counselled part-time in an FE college. In 1973 I was appointed Course Tutor for a Diploma in Counselling at North East London Polytechnic and asked to rewrite the course for a CNAA submission. I experimented with my package of Rogers, Carkhuff, Gilmore and Ivey and one afternoon in 1975, walking past a bookshop I saw a whole window display of *The Skilled Helper* (Egan, 1975). Opening it, I found all my bits and pieces – or nearly all – neatly combined in Egan's model.

The model was exciting because it demystified the process of counselling, setting out three stages: (1) helping clients explore; (2) helping them come to a deeper understanding; and (3) helping them to plan and act. Each stage defined specific skills needed by the counsellor – and the client; the first stage skills which help the client to explore were the same skills which communicate the core qualities and so help to build a working relationship. The second stage skills, which challenge the client to begin to move inward, were those defined by Carkhuff, except Egan added 'deeper empathy' – being able to communicate what the client is not quite in touch with (the music behind the words). This skill, with the others, helps clients come to new understandings of themselves. Egan's third stage skills are creative ways of helping clients plan and implement some action to become more effective in managing their lives.

So, I found this a useful model for my own counselling, for teaching the diploma and also, very importantly, for the short courses we were developing for other professionals who wanted to use counselling skills in their work. With Hazel Johns I promoted this model in the series of programmes *Principles of Counselling* we did for the BBC in the late 1970s (Inskipp and Johns, 1983). I used this model in writing *Counselling: The Trainer's Handbook* (Inskipp, 1986) and in the open learning course *Counselling Skills* (Inskipp, 1988). I still use Egan's original model in designing and teaching courses in counselling skills. I am not happy with the models he has developed in his third and fourth editions[1] and think probably his most useful model is that outlined in *People in Systems* which he wrote with Michael Cowan (Egan and Cowan, 1979).

In my counselling I find Egan's model a useful map to find my way with a client – especially if I feel lost. His first stage skills are my essential building blocks throughout my work, and I become more convinced of their importance the more I counsel, supervise and train. The model also allows me to use an 'integrated' mode of counselling especially in his stage 2, 'helping the client come to a deeper understanding', where I can call on a range of theories and techniques which may be useful with different individual clients. I also like his emphasis on working from a healthy model of personality rather than a pathological one – a developmental model which identifies the *stages* and *tasks* of life, the *skills* needed for the tasks and the *systems* in which the person develops, which either help or hinder development.

This brings me to psychosynthesis and the other thread of my life which led me there. In my 20s I became estranged from the Christian church and the beliefs in which I had been reared and started a search for the meaning and purpose of life. This led me to train as a biologist and to explore Sufism, Buddhism, to read philosophy and a wide selection of New Age literature. In 1981 as I was taking early retirement from the Polytechnic, I attended a workshop at a BAC Conference on Psychosynthesis and found I liked the emphasis on looking at human beings from a trans-personal perspective which stresses that humans have a spirit or soul as well as a body, mind and emotions, and which advocates working with all four parts in counselling. It took me several years before I attended a week's course on 'The Essentials of Psychosyn-thesis' and then decided in 1988 at the age of 68 to take a 3-year Diploma.

What has psychosynthesis given me beyond Egan?

It has given me a wider vision of myself and my universe, some clues to meaning and purpose of life, alternative ways to understand human development and some of the blocks to development. Also it has given me additional tools – techniques and methods with which I can work and share with clients ways to help them create their lives with more meaning and joy. I will try and expand on these.

Assagioli (1965), the founder of psychosynthesis, trained originally with Freud but become disenchanted with Freud's 'depth psychology' and proposed a 'height psychology' which did not ignore the lower unconscious of past memories and stored emotions but recognized humans as receiving energies which are noble and creative from the transpersonal or higher unconscious. This equates with and extends my humanistic view received from Rogers.

I see clients – and all people – as being on a journey, motivated towards some inner purpose which the journey is to discover. Life is a process of 'becoming'. Life events are ways we can use to develop ourselves, to attune ourselves to an inner voice which will guide us towards the meaning and purpose of life. Some clients come searching, with a longing for life to be more deeply fulfilling, others come wanting relief of pain, to sort out confusion, to make choices or changes. I do not push my philosophy and I work with them where they are, but hold a transpersonal view as a working framework. I am often asking myself 'What transpersonal qualities are trying to emerge in this person?' as well as 'How are the patterns in their life blocking them?' and, from Egan, 'How are the systems they live in, and lack of lifeskills holding them back?' Problems are not simply pathological states to be eliminated, but rather indicators of a hidden thrust towards integration.

Psychosynthesis by its name means synthesis of the parts into a whole. A main aim is to synthesize the multiple aspects of the individual – sub-personalities – around a personal centre, a 'self', and then to effect a greater synthesis between the personal 'self' and the transpersonal 'Self'. I find working with the concept of sub-personalities fascinating and useful – to help clients identify the different parts of themselves which have a life of their own, then to learn to disidentify from their 'critic', their 'juggler', their 'sad child' to build the 'self' as a conductor of this orchestra of sub-personalities – all this enhances my work with clients.

For much of this work I use visualization or guided imagery and this feels a creative way in which to work. Encouraging clients to work in images or symbols seems to have a power to promote change which often words cannot have. Visualizing their sad inner child sub-personalities, getting to know them, talking with them to find out their needs, going back into painful situations, experiencing the pain with them, then comforting and loving them, all this can heal parts words cannot reach. Psychosynthesis also uses many Gestalt techniques for separation and integration, identifying projections and building awareness of emotions and bodily sensations, helping clients see the bigger picture of their lives (Whitmore, 1991).

So, psychosynthesis has brought me new ways of being and new ways of working – and Egan is still important to me. In fact, I have brought Egan to psychosynthesis; I now teach his model in the Counselling Skills Module of the Psychosynthesis Diploma. A good synthesis for me!

Note

1   I find the models, ideas and language Egan uses in his third and fourth editions are confusing and complex – I prefer the simplicity and clarity of his early models.

References

Assagioli, Roberto (1965) *Psychosynthesis: A Manual of Principles and Techniques*. London: Turnstone Books.

Carkhuff, Robert (1969) *Helping and Human Relations*, Vol. 1. New York: Holt, Rinehart & Winston.

Egan, Gerard (1975) *The Skilled Helper* (1st edn). Monterey, CA: Brooks/Cole.

Egan, Gerard and Cowan, Michael (1979) *People in Systems*. Monterey, CA: Brooks/Cole.

Gilmore, Susan (1973) *The Counsellor in Training*. New Jersey: Prentice Hall.

Inskipp, Francesca (1986) *Counselling: The Trainer's Handbook*. Cambridge: National Extension College.

Inskipp, Francesca (1988) *Counselling Skills*. Cambridge: National Extension College.

Inskipp, Francesca and Johns, Hazel (1983) *Principles of Counselling: 4 casettes with notes, Series I and II*. St Leonards-on-Sea: Alexia Publications.

Rogers, Carl (1975) *On Becoming a Person*. Boston: Houghton Mifflin.

Whitmore, Diana (1991) *Psychosynthesis Counselling in Action*. London: Sage.

19 Towards a personal model of counselling

What factors do I need to consider in developing a personal model of counselling?

Jenifer Elton Wilson

This question is one that returns to haunt thoughtful counsellors throughout their professional careers. Whatever our training experience or theoretical allegiance may be, we aspire to achieve some level of personal authenticity in our work with clients. Basic training in 'active listening' skills all emphasize the need to search for the real thoughts and emotions behind spoken words. We are taught to listen to our own inner reactions while observing those of our clients. These responses are shaped by our current belief system, some of which may still be unvoiced, wrapped in the protective shell of our feelings and our intuitions. Our choice of theoretical orientation, no matter how broadly described, is one way in which we are articulating these beliefs. A 'personal model' is the label attached to the explanations we give for what brought our clients to seek a counsellor's help and for how the interaction between client and counsellor can bring about change.

My own interest in this need to make personal sense of the *what* and the *how* of psychological change led me to offer workshops on the search for an individually meaningful theory to groups of counsellors, psychotherapists and psychologists. In this response, I hope to convey some of the processes and outcomes of the deep self-questioning and brain-storming which pervaded these short events. I invite readers to ask themselves the same difficult questions and to compare their answers first with the model of counselling in which they were trained and then with the explanations given by other approaches. The definitions given are a synthesis of the work done by participants and my own current understanding of the major theoretical assumptions.

Before any attempt to plumb the basic tenets which shape our professional activities, we need to consider the pragmatic influences on our choice of counselling model. These choices are almost inevitably shaped by the setting in which we work or in which we are still being trained. What is the culturally permitted paradigm to which we are conforming? A career as a counsellor is often fraught with the difficulty of finding jobs or places to practice. While it is rare for a work setting to stipulate one particular theoretically based approach, there is often a generally accepted model of counselling which is considered politically or culturally correct. Educational institutions generally favour a humanistic approach, commercial employers and medical settings tend to favour a problem-solving cognitive-behavioural approach while retaining some reverence for a psychoanalytic knowledge base. There is a more or less subtle conditioning to conform.

Our first choice of a model of counselling

Ideally, we were free to choose our basic training as counsellors, although even this decision is likely to have been limited by financial considerations and by the availability of training in the vicinity. There is an inevitable authority and power in that first choice which is likely still to be influencing our thinking. A majority of counsellors, in contrast with psychotherapists, commence their engagement with the counselling profession by undertaking a basic skills training. The theoretical explanation depends on the *language* used to describe the development of counselling skills in our first training course. Rogerian trainers accentuate the empowerment experienced through the congruent expression of our real selves. Psychodynamic trainers emphasize the relief expressed as we own up to the deep reality of the unconscious motivation. Cognitive-behavioural trainers encourage constructive action, free from the exaggerations of irrational thought.

The first factor we need now to *reconsider* is the continuing influence of our earliest substantial training experience. A match was found between the ideology we then espoused and the model of counselling by which we were most heavily influenced. Perhaps we attended an exciting workshop, read an inspiring book or chose the same training route as our own counsellor. The approach we used to our clients was shaped by these first theoretical explanations, and any successes we achieved were ascribed to the efficacy of the methods and techniques recommended by this model.

From early conceptual clarity to strategic eclecticism

The general movement, within counselling and psychotherapy, towards eclecticism is nearly always client-driven. The counsellor's original choice of theoretical orientation with its accompanying methods and training reflects a personal understanding of some basic values. Clients bring needs, problems and symptoms framed by their own meanings and values. Examples of a clash of values abound. A man seeks practical help for a perceived failure in sexual potency from a counsellor who believes that the only answer to this problem is the achievement of an intimate and authentic relationship. An elderly Asian woman struggles between her need to please her husband and her wish to understand the feminist consciousness raising of her counsellor. A physically abusing parent insists that his aim in seeing a counsellor is solely to 'know' himself better. The counsellor is forced into a more pragmatic re-frame.

> *What* treatment, by *whom*, is most effective for *this* individual with *that* specific problem, and under *which* set of circumstances? (Paul, 1967)

The client–counsellor dyad is set within professional limitations and influenced by the beliefs attached to that setting. Societal values impinge through the family system of client and counsellor, both of whom may hold unexpressed political convictions. All these variables lead to the erosion of the counsellor's original theoretical clarity and a sense of losing touch with a personal world-view.

Fundamental questions for the counsellor

It is with this sense of an overload of conflicting influences and pressures, that counsellors and psychotherapists have arrived at the workshops on a 'personal theory of meaning'. A few of these participants have a simpler need. Like some readers of this response, they are seeking information in order to make an informed choice with regard to training. In any case, all share a sense of uncertainty and confusion which is uncomfortable but creative, an essential component of professional development. I invite them, as I now invite the reader, to take themselves back to the *ideas* about counselling which first attracted them to the profession whether this happened ten or twenty years ago, or last year.

Consider the following questions.

Question 1 What do most people search for in their lives?
Question 2 How is 'personality' formed and how can children be helped to develop healthy personalities?
Question 3 How does human unhappiness lead to problematic behaviour?
Question 4 How can the counsellor help the client towards making effective changes?

	Cognitive behavioural	Psychoanalytic	Existential-humanistic
	Rational-Emotive, Beck's Cognitive, Personal Construct and Egan's models of counselling	Freudian, Jungian, Bio-energetic and Kleinian models of counselling	Transactional Analysis, Gestalt and Person-Centred models of counselling
Q.1 Human aim	To function as a reasonably happy and rational human being in a social world, able to problem solve without catastrophizing.	To move from unconscious despair towards being fully able to love, to work and to accept difficulty and bereavement.	To be fully authentic and responsible; and to achieve self-actualization congruent with individual potential.
Q.2 Personal development	Through learnt patterns of behaviour, which are affectively and consistently reinforced. Health depends on realistic positive conditioning which takes into account social systems and temperamental differences.	Through the type of resolution achieved between survival needs, sensual gratification and the real demands of social relationship. Health depends on achieving a balanced level of containment.	Through the conditions of worth applied throughout our lives. Health springs from the amount of warmth, respect, acceptance and empowerment experienced, and the development of courage to be.
Q.3 Route to pain	An over-determined construction of perceived reality which leads to patterns of maladaptive responses.	The continuity of trauma through the unconscious power of transference and counter-transference.	The need for self-protection, the lack of personal value or self-worth, and the fear of uncertainty and annihilation.
Q.4 Task of the counsellor	By exploring patterns of thinking, suggesting experiments in behaviour change, and challenging irrational emotional reactions.	By encouraging insight into unconscious links with significant, past relationships providing a reparative and reality-based emotional experience.	By trusting the process of the client and providing a real relationship of unconditional positive regard, facilitative of responsible adult behaviour.

First step
What would be the answers given by your *original* model of counselling? Try and get back into that frame of reference, perhaps remembering your original trainers and supervisors. This can be a revealing and sometimes disturbing exercise.

Answer 1 ....
Answer 2 ....
Answer 3 ....
Answer 4 ....

Second step
Now ask *yourself* the same questions, and answer them from the theoretical frame with which you now feel comfortable. How have your original concepts survived?

Answer 1 ....
Answer 2 ....
Answer 3 ....
Answer 4 ....

The table opposite gives some of the answers arrived at by groups of counsellors and psychotherapists working together. The first three questions attempt to *explain* the human condition and the roots of distress while the last question looks for *solutions*.

Three main orientations are given, and linked with my own suggestions as to the models of counselling which have taken their major influence from each overarching theoretical framework. Inevitably there is some overlap, and not all readers will agree with the 'family placement' I have proposed. Some workshop participants have disputed the grouping of Egan and Personal Construct Psychology under a cognitive-behavioural umbrella. My own difficulty is with Transactional Analysis which seems to me to draw from all three main orientations equally. A more extensive table comparing theoretical approaches of the major orientations can be found in the final chapter in Ivey et al. (1987).

Towards a personal integration

All the 'personal theory of meaning' workshops I have facilitated have revealed the extent of integration which is now taking place between models of counselling. The tension between what is pragmatically possible, given a particular setting, and what is needed by a range of clients is being inventively and radically responded to by many counsellors and psychotherapists. They look to other approaches to broaden their own understanding and bring variety to their interactions with their clients. Inevitably, a shift to eclecticism can bring with it confusion and uncertainty. Intellectual clarification is one way of grounding our experiments as practitioners into an integrated whole.

I suggest that there are three levels at which we engage with theoretical concepts in our profession as counsellors. At the level of *behaviour*, most counsellors are constrained by their own particular style of interpersonal interaction. No matter how strongly an analytically trained counsellor believes in the importance of a neutral and reticent approach, a warm engaging personality is likely to evoke a matching response in clients, resulting in sessions which video recording would reveal as more closely resembling the work of a person-centred counsellor. Similarly, attempts to work actively and encourage full blown catharsis will fall flat if the counsellor is temperamentally cool and restrained in manner. During the early stages of professional development, most practitioners limit themselves to a known range of techniques. A more experienced counsellor is likely to feel confident and relaxed enough to experiment outside the tenets of their particular model of counselling.

While the wise counsellor maintains a personally comfortable mode of interaction, it is at the level of *conscious thought* that the meaning of the counselling session is understood and concepts generated. An honest struggle with the questions suggested above can reveal a theoretical position which may challenge our allegiance to a particular orientation. An occasional re-frame of our conceptual standpoint can enlighten and refresh our work, especially when we feel stuck.

These temporary reconstructions of our perceived reality will only create a permanent metamorphosis in meaning making if they resonate with our deepest *belief systems*. It is to these that we return and with which we must sincerely struggle in order to retain the authenticity which will communicate itself to our clients. To hold on to a set of political or spiritual allegiances which no longer ring true is a sure path to professional burn-out for the counsellor.

At any stage of professional development, it can be useful for counsellors to attempt to define themselves as follows:

In my counselling sessions I use the approach of
....
....

I think about my work through the concepts of

....

....

My philosophical belief system is shaped by the views of

....

....

The table on page 98 can be used to sharpen and define this analysis. For example, my own counselling *approach* is usually actively explorative of the patterns of interaction taking place between my client and myself (see psychoanalytic answer to question 4, column 2). As I do this, I am *thinking* about the client's original strategy for survival, how this is being repeated both inside and outside the counselling session and what type of reparative experience does this client need to move through this impasse (see psychoanalytically based answers to questions 2 and 3, column 2). However my style as a practitioner and my theorizing is now grounded in an existential-humanistic *belief* in the transformational potential of the client's own willingness to accept and experience the risky business of living a life of increased authenticity (existentialist-humanistic answer to question 1, column 3).

I suggest you work though your theoretical self-definition alone and then talk it through with a professional colleague whom you trust and who knows your work, preferably someone who has had access to audio or video recordings of your sessions with clients. If two or more models of counselling are included in the answers, ask yourself whether this demonstrates a considered integration or a gradual drift towards a loss of theoretical consistency. Richard Wessler has written with honesty and pain of his own realization of

> recognising privately and publicly that I have been doing something else for a good number of years. Also the dilemma concerning my attempts to put some label to what I have been doing, and letting other people know about this too. (Wessler, in Dryden, 1985: 82–5)

For most of us a realization of inconsistency between theory and practice does not lead us to risk professional isolation and ostracization, as in Wessler's case. Instead, our struggles towards our own theoretical clarity and consistency can continue to revive the excitement we felt in our original choice to become counsellors.

References

Dryden, W. (1985) *Therapists' Dilemmas*. London: Harper & Row.

Ivey, A.E., Ivey, M.B. and Simek-Downing, L. (1987) *Counseling and Psychotherapy: Integrating Skills, Theory and Practice*. New Jersey: Prentice-Hall.

Paul, G. (1967) 'Strategy of outcome research in psychotherapy', *Journal of Consulting Psychology*, 31: 109–18.

PART FIVE

ETHICAL ISSUES

---

20 Counsellor/client sex

*The BAC Code of Ethics and Practice just says that
it is unethical for counsellors to have sex with their
clients. This means that it wouldn't be unethical for
a counsellor to end their counselling relationship
with a client one minute and have sex with that
person the next minute. Given this, wouldn't it be
better to safeguard the well-being of clients if the
BAC Code was more stringent in this regard? I am
thinking of certain codes which prohibit
counsellors ever having sexual relations with
people who have been their clients. Can you
please comment.*

Tim Bond

The issue of sexual relations between counsellors and former clients
is one which is being hotly debated by counsellors. The passion
that is aroused is not merely because sexual issues evoke strong
personal opinions in British culture. This is an issue which draws
attention to differences between different schools of counselling. I
would therefore like to provide a two part answer to your question.
First, I will outline the current provisions of the British Association
for Counselling's *Code of Ethics and Practice for Counsellors*
which have recently changed from the position described in your
question. These recent changes have been in response to a
particular pragmatic problem and are therefore very limited in their
scope and do not adequately deal with the major issues raised by
this topic. In the second part of my answer I will try to outline
what these issues are.

First, a new provision was adopted by the Annual General
Meeting of the BAC in September 1992. This states:

> Counsellors must not exploit clients financially, sexually, emotionally or in any other way. Engaging in sexual activity with current clients or within 12 weeks of the end of the counselling relationship is unethical.
>
> If the counselling relationship has been over an extended period of time or been working in-depth, a much longer 'cooling off' period is required and a life-time prohibition on future sexual relationship with the client may be more appropriate.

This new provision was created to solve a specific problem which had arisen in the Complaints Procedure. Since 1984, there has been a clear prohibition on sex between counsellors and their current clients. However, there have been instances of counsellors seeking to avoid complaints by clients about their sexual behaviour with them by arguing that they were no longer their clients and therefore whatever had happened fell outside the provisions of the code. This argument was valid on a strict interpretation of the words. The previous form of words, as your question pointed out, permits someone to end their counselling relationship one minute and have sex with that person the next. Although I do not know of any situation where this has actually happened so quickly, I am aware of a few instances where sex may have started later the same day or within a week of the ending of the counselling. In the new requirements, a time lapse of twelve weeks was chosen as the minimum time which would provide time for reflection and second thoughts by both people and, for the purpose of the Complaints Procedure, created a sufficient division between what is within the counselling relationship and what might be considered to fall outside it. When this was discussed at the Annual General Meeting, there was a majority view that a 'cooling off period' is desirable, but most argued for either a much longer cooling off period or a total prohibition on sex with former clients. Some voted against this new measure because they fear that it is inappropriate because it attempts to cover too many disparate situations within one provision. As things stand, it is unlikely that the new section in the code will have a long life. It is likely to be revised again within the next two years, but in the meantime it will serve to close an automatic escape clause for the small numbers of counsellors who may have engaged in sexually inappropriate behaviour and it will certainly help focus the debate on an important issue for counsellors. At this stage in the development of counselling I believe we still have a great deal to learn about what constitutes sexually appropriate and inappropriate behaviour by counsellors. It is something which we need to explore and educate ourselves about because clients who are subjected to inappropriate behaviour are often severely distressed and it is one of the situations where they would have been in a better position if they had never received any counselling.

In the second part of my answer, I would like to highlight some of the issues which require more consideration by contrasting two hypothetical examples. The first example is:

> Sarah has sought counselling over a challenging situation at work in order to receive some personal support and some assistance with a decision about her future career. She feels a strong personal liking for her counsellor and twelve weeks after the three counselling sessions it took to resolve the issue are completed, she invites her counsellor out for a meal. After several social meetings a friendship has developed and they have discussed a strong sexual attraction towards each other. What should they do?

This scenario describes a situation in which two people have deliberately sought to maintain a clear distinction between their counselling relationship and a potential sexual relationship. Only when the counselling has been completed do they wish to start a sexual relationship on the basis of a carefully made decision which each has made autonomously. The gender of the counsellor has been left ambiguous because the issue of sexual orientation is irrelevant. It does not make any ethical difference whether the proposed relationship is homosexual or heterosexual. The crucial issue is whether or not the counsellor should have the possibility of this potentially positive relationship and on what terms without compromising her/his professional reputation as a counsellor.

At this stage in the discussion it is possible to identify a division of opinion amongst counsellors which roughly corresponds to whether or not they belong to a psychodynamic approach to counselling. Those who belong to other traditions appear more willing to consider the possibility of the proposed relationship subject to a number of safeguards, such as the lapse of an adequate period of time for independent and careful decision-making, the counsellor consulting her/his counselling supervisor, and a clear understanding about a prohibition on them resuming the counselling relationship. On the other hand, there are alternative psychodynamic views which emphasize the possibility of a transferential relationship persisting beyond the formal end of the counselling role and perhaps having an unrecognized influence on either the client or counsellor or both, which means that the decision to enter into a sexual relationship only *seems* to be that between autonomous adults but the psychological reality is possibly better understood in terms of child–parent. What is proposed is analogous to an adult woman and her parent saying they can put their parent–child relationship behind them and feel free to enter into a sexual relationship on equal terms, something which is impossible to achieve from most points of view. Those who take the view that the analogy is an exact one strongly favour a life-time prohibition of sexual contact with former clients. Others take the view that the analogy is not inevitable but depends on the actual dynamics in the counsellor–client relationship and perhaps a future sexual relationship could be countenanced, provided a child–parent-like transference has not been evoked in the counselling or has been resolved. The duration, depth and intensity of the counselling relationship might all have to be taken into account in the assessment of whether or not a transference has occurred. A decision about the appropriateness of a future sexual relationship would depend on these deliberations.

The first example considered people wanting to enter sexual relationship for positive reasons. The second example looks at the darker side of counsellor–client relationships.

> Bob is a counsellor who has difficulty in establishing personal relationships. He realizes that in the past he has played with fire by having sex with current clients and has therefore decided in the future he will terminate the counselling relationship with anyone he wants sex with in order to offer friendship in the hope of a sexual encounter. He will conceal his real reasons for his actions from his clients.

In these circumstances there is no attempt to create a situation in which both people are acting autonomously. The intention is to entrap the client to satisfy the counsellor's personal needs. Situations of this kind appear to apply more frequently to male counsellors than female, but not invariably. So far, no-one has sought to defend this kind of exploitation of clients. Most counsellors would be very concerned about this level of exploitation and would be even more concerned if the perpetrator moved from manipulation to actual physical coercion and actual abuse of former clients. In practice, this latter situation is likely to provide the client with opportunities for legal remedies as well as professional sanctions against the counsellor in a way which a less abusive but equally psychologically damaging exploitation might not.

Your question asks me to comment on whether I think it is appropriate to become more stringent about sex with former clients. Although I can only speak for myself at this early stage in initiating discussion of this topic within the BAC, my view is that it is appropriate for the BAC to become more stringent than the current requirements. The challenge will be to find a way which permits a relationship to develop between adults who have previously been in a counselling relationship when it is appropriate in the circumstances of the first example and to prevent the exploitation of clients in situations like the second. If, in addition, you take the view that not all counselling relationships create a power relationship or transference which lasts the client's life-time, the regulation of relationships between counsellors and clients will need to take this into account. The regulations will need to be appropriately protective of clients' interests but without infantilizing them or ignoring their right to act autonomously once the counsellor–client relationship is truly ended.

21 Reporting a colleague's misconduct

If I were to learn that a counsellor colleague was having sex with one of his clients, what should I do?

Tim Bond

This is a situation which should not be ignored. The potential seriousness of sexual exploitation of clients justifies overcoming a reluctance to intrude, a fear of challenging and a risk of personal embarrassment. Members of the British Association for Counselling have long taken the view that to engage in sexual activity with current clients is both unethical and exploitative (BAC, 1984, 1990, 1992). This standard has been adopted for a number of reasons. First, there is an inequality of power between the client and counsellor inherent in one 'being helped' and the other acting as 'helper' which leaves the client vulnerable to manipulation or to more subtle but equally powerful ways of being influenced. Second, psychoanalytically trained counsellors have pointed out how the transference dynamic between the counsellor and client may undermine the client's capacity to choose whether to engage in sex on an adult-to-adult basis because emotionally the client is in the position of child–adult or child–parent. When this occurs the counsellor is in effect reparenting the client, a relationship which can be extremely constructive, but if it is abused by entering into a sexual relationship with the client, then emotionally it is experienced by clients as sexual abuse. This may explain an American research finding that clients who have reported sexual relationships with their counsellors experience the same kind of psychological distress as the victim of rape or child sexual abuse (Pope, 1988). Third, counselling requires a relationship in which boundaries are maintained in order to allow the client to discuss intimate and personal concerns without crossing over into a sexual relationship. The psychological self-exposure and vulnerability of clients in counselling requires the same level of sexual abstinence that doctors give their patients because of their physical vulnerability. This is essential not only to establishing trust with individual clients but also the trust and respect of the wider

community. When counsellors have sex with their clients it is not
only a matter of the damage they can cause the client directly
involved, which can be considerable, but also the damage caused
to the reputation of counselling as a whole.

The circumstances in which you learn about your colleague
having sex with one of his clients will be highly relevant to what
you do next. Therefore, I would like to consider a number of these
which I know have occurred in actual practice.

For example:

> You are at a social event when someone approaches you and
> asks if you have heard about the rumour that your colleague is
> having sex with a client. You respond that you have not heard
> this and your informant tells you that the rumour is widely
> believed and there are circumstantial details which appear to
> make it credible.

A manifestly ill-founded or malicious rumour could properly be
ignored although out of respect for your colleague you might wish
to inform him of the existence of the rumour. The dilemma of the
situation described in the example is that there could be a basis of
truth behind the rumour but you cannot be certain. Alternatively,
you may already have your suspicions and the rumour has added
weight to them. In either of these circumstances I think it is essential to raise the issue with your colleague directly. Any further
action that you take will depend on his response. If he denies that
there is any truth in the rumour and you believe him, it may be
appropriate to support him in counteracting the rumour. On the
other hand, if the denial is not totally convincing, you may have
to use your own judgment about how to find out what is really
going on or decide to await further developments. If your colleague
admits to the relationship, you are in a position similar to the next
example:

> You are approached by your colleague who admits to having a
> sexual relationship with a client. He asks you what should he
> do.

If your colleague is asking for help over the issue and he is willing
to raise the issue of his behaviour with his counselling supervisor
and his counselling associates, your role is to encourage him in this
course of action and to consider the needs of the client. The
client's emotional state may determine whether she (or he) wishes
to be referred to another counsellor or to make contact with
organizations which specialize in supporting clients who have been
sexually exploited by their therapists. The addresses of two

organizations can be found at the end of this section. Occasionally the client may be feeling better about what has occurred than the counsellor. I am aware of two situations described in British literature on this subject (Thorne, 1987; Russell, 1993) where the client appears to have benefited from sexual activity with the counsellor, but these are exceptions in comparison with the much larger incidence of distressed clients. Brian Thorne discusses his experience of one of these situations on pages 113–17.[1]

A number of issues will need careful consideration if the sexual relationship has not already ceased before you learn about it. In most circumstances, it is highly desirable to consider the possibility of ending the counselling relationship by referring the client to another counsellor acceptable to her (or him). It is difficult to disentangle the dual relationship causing only the minimum of distress. The potential vulnerability of the client in this situation needs to be taken into account and given priority. It may be one of those rare situations where the client needs to be offered the opportunity to be seen by someone who is independent of the counselling relationship to help her (or him) determine the best way forward. The counselling supervisor, yourself or someone else may be most suitable for this role. It is important that the way this is handled does not unnecessarily add to the distress experienced by the client. She (or he) may already have had personal interests made subservient to the counsellor's and there is the risk that the client's vulnerability will be overlooked again in the concern about the professional issues involved and the consequences for the counsellor. If, in the process of disentangling this situation, a conflict between the needs of the client and the counsellor becomes apparent, it is the client's needs that ought to be given priority.

If you learn of the sexual relationship between a counsellor and a client during a counselling session, the issue of confidentiality requires careful consideration. For example:

> A client comes to tell you about her relationship with your colleague but she cannot bear the emotional turbulence it is caus-ing her and has decided to end it. She is afraid this will distress your colleague and asks you to be supportive of him.

In these circumstances the wishes of the client with regard to confidentiality ought to be given priority. It is possible that the harm done to the client personally or professionally by any breach of confidentiality by yourself could be considerable and this needs to be taken into account. Nonetheless it is important that the client is presented with the possibility of taking up a complaint against a counsellor with either his employer or a counselling association or, alternatively, supporting you in taking up such a complaint. It may be the client will only consent to you taking up the issue with the counsellor privately. This is better than doing nothing but it is less satisfactory then having the whole situation investigated more fully by a professional body.

It will be apparent from this selection of possible examples in which the situation you suggest could arise, that the priority of your concerns should be the client, professional issues and the counsellor, in that order. What this will mean in actual practice will vary according to the actual circumstances. In my opinion, it is important that the circumstances of the sexual relationship ought to be raised for consideration by the counsellor's professional association. Usually this is only possible with the client's consent unless you have direct knowledge of what occurred, perhaps because of what the counsellor concerned has told you. If the client is very distressed, it may be some considerable time before she (or he) feels able to participate in these proceedings. A time lapse of several years is not unusual. In both the USA and UK, the usual consequences for counsellors who have sexually exploited counsellors is expulsion from membership. However, in my opinion, the penalty ought to take into account the actual harm suffered by clients and sometimes a period of working under close supervision or a period of suspension may be more appropriate.

In the United States there is some pioneering work taking place to offer treatment to therapists who have sex with clients. It will be some time before we are in a position to provide a similar service in Britain. At the moment we are only beginning to understand the consequences of sex between counsellors and clients from the client's perspective.

Note

1. As discussed in his answer on pp. 113–17, Brian Thorne refutes absolutely that his behaviour constituted sexual activity (Ed.).

References

BAC (1984, 1990, 1992) *Code of Ethics and Practice for Counsellors*. Rugby: British Association for Counselling.

Pope, K.S. (1988) 'How clients are harmed by sexual contact with mental health professionals: The syndrome and its prevalence', *Journal of Counseling and Development*, 67: 222–6.

Russell, J. (1993) *Out of Bounds: Sexual Exploitation in Counselling and Therapy*. London: Sage.

Thorne, B. (1987) 'Beyond the core conditions', in Windy Dryden (ed.), *Key Cases in Psychotherapy*. London: Croom Helm, also published in B. Thorne (1991) *Person-Centred Counselling – Therapeutic and Spiritual Dimensions*. London: Whurr Publishers.

Addresses of organizations offering support to clients who have been sexually exploited by counsellors and therapists

Abuse in Therapy Support Network
c/o Women's Support Project
871 Springfield Road
Glasgow G31 4HZ
(Please send stamped addressed envelope. Welcomes enquiries from men and women. Runs women only groups.)

POPAN (Prevention of Professional Abuse Network)
Flat 1
20 Daleham Gardens
London NW3 5DA
(Please enclose an SAE with a small contribution with correspondence if possible as the project is currently unfunded. All enquiries are welcome although there may be a delay in replying at times.)

22 Body and spirit

I have read your case in Windy Dryden's edited book entitled Key Cases in Psychotherapy *where you describe your work with a client, which culminated in a nude embrace between the two of you. While I understand the context in which this happened and the therapeutic value it had for your client, nevertheless, I still consider that, by your actions, you were in breach of the BAC* Code of Ethics and Practice *with respect to counsellors not engaging in sexual activity with their clients. Can you comment on this?*

Brian Thorne

I am aware that before I can have any hope of responding to your question there is a need to fill in the background. Let me acknowledge from the outset that the description of my 'key case' in Windy Dryden's edited book has been the cause of more comment, correspondence and general discussion than almost anything else I have ever written and there are times when I wish I had been more cowardly (or less foolhardy) and never set pen to paper (Thorne, 1987). Having said that, I welcome this opportunity to revisit the terrain that my client, Sally, and I explored together and to attempt to throw more light on some of the issues involved. It is perhaps worth noting, incidentally, that almost all the correspondence I have received about this notorious chapter has been overwhelmingly positive. One further point which needs to be noted is that the work with Sally took place between 1979 and 1983, that is before the 1984 BAC *Code of Ethics* which first prohibited sexual activity with clients. I could not in any case have been in breach of something which at that time did not exist.

Despite my occasional fantasy that the whole country knows about my relationship with Sally in detail, I am modest enough to assume that most of the readers of this book will know nothing of it whatsoever. Briefly, then, Sally was a married client with grave sexual problems with whom I worked for a period of some three years at the beginning of the 1980s. She was the wife of a priest and the couple originally came to see me together after many years of ineffective marital therapy with other practitioners including psychiatrists. They had chosen me because they already knew me socially, had read much of my published work and, most importantly, because I shared their Christian perception of reality. Although Sally quickly came into individual therapy with me, her husband, Kenneth, was kept fully informed of our work throughout its process and both he and the couple's children were actively involved at certain crucial stages. When the 'key case' came to be written up both Sally and Kenneth were fully involved in its composition.

As I explain in the chapter itself, my work with Sally took me into uncharted territory and I am still, ten years later, awe-struck by the extraordinary nature of our therapeutic journey. Without doubt it was a milestone in my personal and professional development and my work since owes much to the discoveries made at that time. Most relevant to your question is the fact that during the course of therapy Sally discovered that she had no option but to allow herself to regress to earlier experience and ultimately to intra-uterine pain. What is more, despite initial shame and terror, she chose to do some of this work either partially or completely unclothed while seeking my co-operation in holding her and, on occasion, in applying gentle massage to various parts of her body. Clearly such work was only undertaken after the most careful review of its implications and, indeed, after a referral to a female therapist trained in body work (which I am not) who was wise enough to see that she could not exonerate me from undertaking a task which belonged to the relationship between Sally and me and could not conveniently be transferred elsewhere.

You will know from your reading of the 'key case' that Sally was (and is) a beautiful woman and that I understandably experienced sexual feelings towards her. My dilemma was whether these feelings could be put at the service of the therapeutic work and thus integrated into my response to her in such a way that she could experience my integrity and thus be encouraged to trust her own. It was here that our shared Christian understanding and the involvement of her husband were so crucial. It rapidly became apparent that if I was to be of real use to Sally I needed to have the deepest possible love for her as a person and to be free to exercise that love in the service of her healing. Essentially, then, my work with Sally became a matter of *soul* loving because both she and I (and Kenneth) believed that the deepest part of the person is the indwelling spirit or soul where God is to be found. But to love Sally as an immortal soul meant a total willingness to accept her as an incarnate being in all her emotionality, physicality and sexuality. What is more this could only be done if I could be confident that my own sexuality was sufficiently integrated within my own being that there was no danger of my abusing Sally or Kenneth or my own wife by moving across boundaries into a relationship where sexuality assumed the primacy. Without doubt there was a risk involved in all this but I would submit that there are few therapeutic relationships of depth where risks are not involved. In this instance our shared Christian allegiance, the involvement of Kenneth and the deepening sense of mutuality between us were, I believe, more than adequate safeguards.

It is within this overall context that the incident of the naked embrace referred to in your question has to be considered. It should be remembered, too, that this event occurred very near the end of therapy and at a stage when a deep mutuality had existed between us for some time. For Sally the moment was critical: for perhaps the first time she was experiencing the full flow of her sexual and creative energy and she was terrified that she would not be able to control it. What is more, she feared she would be destroyed by it and do much evil in the process. My behaviour – and the original text indicates the immense tension I experienced within me during those few moments – was a direct response to her overwhelming fear both of fragmentation and of corruption. By risking my own naked vulnerability and trusting my own integrity I hoped to convey to Sally that she need not fear her sexuality and that her ethical self, based as it was on a deep love of souls, would ensure that her sexuality would confirm her loving rather than corrupt it into lust. It is perhaps not unimportant that I was proved right.

My direct response, therefore, to your question is that in my naked embrace of Sally I was not engaging in sexual activity. For me to do so in a relationship is to seek pleasure in sexual behaviour or to incite the other to seek such pleasure: it involves a deliberate attempt to engage in activity which will arouse sexual feelings in oneself or the other so that these feelings can subsequently be consummated through intercourse or other forms of sexual satisfaction. My naked embrace of Sally was in many ways the antithesis of such behaviour. As a statement it conveyed the message:

> It is possible for a man and woman who love each other and who are attracted to each other sexually to be naked and vulnerable together without self-betrayal and without betraying others. What is more such vulnerability by challenging the tyrannical primacy of sexual desire can hasten integration and spiritual growth.

In the last analysis, I suppose, the credibility of my answer to your question depends to a large extent on whether or not you accept the belief that, at the deepest level, we are spiritual beings and that our greatest need is for spiritual development. If such a view is unacceptable to you I can imagine that, despite your generous acknowledgement that my behaviour with Sally had therapeutic value for her, you may well still conclude that entering into a naked embrace with her was essentially a sexual activity. All my talk of integration and spiritual growth will perhaps seem to you little more than an elaborate form of self-deception and you will be left with the problem of determining whether I am a benevolent or malevolent self-deceiver. I am aware, incidentally, that the current interpretation of the BAC Code leaves me in one or other of these categories, but I should, of course, wish to challenge strongly that interpretation.

It is of some reassurance to me to know that others more eminent than I have struggled with many of the issues by which I was confronted in my relationship with Sally. In his best-selling book *The Road Less Traveled*, the American psychiatrist Scott Peck has this to say:

> Because of the necessarily long and intimate nature of the psycho-therapeutic relationship, it is inevitable that both patients and therapists routinely develop strong or extremely strong sexual attractions to each other. The pressures to sexually consummate such attractions may be enormous. I suspect that some of those in the profession of psychotherapy who cast stones at a therapist who has related sexually with a patient may not themselves be loving therapists and may not therefore have any real understanding of the enormity of the pressures involved. Moreover, were I ever to have a case in which I concluded after careful and judicious consideration that my patient's spiritual growth would be substantially furthered by our having sexual relations, I would proceed to have them. In fifteen years of practice, however, I have not yet had such a case, and I find it difficult to imagine that such a case could really exist. (Peck, 1979: 175–6)

My own position mirrors Peck's statement almost exactly and it is interesting to note that since writing *The Road Less Traveled* Peck has himself embraced a Christian commitment and presumably now has as much trouble with church attitudes to sexuality as I do. The criterion of the client's spiritual growth remains for me the ultimate and overwhelmingly important issue in the monitoring of my own behaviour as a counsellor. When I took the risk of holding Sally in a naked embrace it was because I believed that in doing so I might enable her spiritual growth to be 'substantially furthered'. For me it was not 'engaging in sexual activity' but a perilous leap of faith undertaken on behalf of a human soul who had shown me such trust that I could be nothing less for her than my total self.

References

Peck, Scott (1979) *The Road Less Traveled: A New Psychology of Love, Traditional Values and Spiritual Growth*. New York: Simon & Schuster.
Thorne, B.J. (1987) 'Beyond the core conditions', in W. Dryden (ed.), *Key Cases in Psychotherapy*. London: Croom Helm.

23 When to protect a client from self-destruction

I am struggling with a dilemma between respecting a client's autonomy and right to choose on the one hand, and protecting that client from self-destruction on the other. In this context, what steps should I, as a counsellor, legitimately take to stop one of my clients from committing suicide?

Tim Bond

The irreversibility of a successful suicide inevitably means that both the client and counsellor are confronting a situation of ultimate seriousness. Some counsellors believe that, despite the potential seriousness of the situation, suicide is the ultimate right of an individual (Laing, 1967) or that even the suicidal remain morally responsible for their own acts (Szasz, 1986) and therefore the principle of respect for the client's choice and autonomy should predominate. Some mental health professionals take an opposite point of view because, in their experience, most suicides are a response to a temporary state of hopelessness. They argue that if someone can be protected from acting on self-destructive urges the will to live returns and the problems which have contributed to the client's state of hopelessness can be dealt with. From this viewpoint all suicides are a tragic waste of life and the principle of preventing self-destruction ought always to predominate. Therefore, coercive methods of preventing suicide are justified. I am aware of counsellors who are certain of the correctness of one or the other of these points of view but I suspect that counsellors who cling exclusively to one opinion or the other do so out of an attempt to control their own anxiety in a potentially extremely anxiety-provoking situation. I believe the choice between respect for the client's right to choose and the need to protect a client from self-destruction cannot be resolved once and for all. Because suicides occur in very different circumstances, the counsellor ought to assess each situation before deciding which of the two principles ought to prevail. Some examples may help to illustrate this opinion.

Audrey has a terminal illness and has for many months asserted her desire to die at home in a way which is under her control rather than face hospitalization or dependency on others. She has discussed her wishes with her family and doctor who have expressed reservations about her planned suicide but she has maintained her point of view over several months.

This is clearly the autonomous intention of someone who has made a deliberate decision and has sustained it over a period of time and there is no evidence of her being pressurized into it. The counsellor may wish to help her review her decision and make sure that it is made with knowledge of any alternatives, including home nursing, the use of a living will in which she states her wishes about the kind of terminal care she wants, or hospice care. However, when all her circumstances are taken into account it seems appropriate to respect her choice. Even if the counsellor wishes actively to support the client's plans, he or she needs to be aware that euthanasia is illegal in Britain and that anyone 'who aids, abets, counsels or procures the suicide of another or an attempt by another to commit suicide, shall be liable on conviction on indictment to imprisonment for a term not exceeding fourteen years' (Suicide Act, 1961, section 2). To 'counsel' in this legal context means to conspire, advise or knowingly give assistance. None of these are activities usually encompassed by counselling as the term is used by BAC.

An alternative example provides the kind of situation which counsellors encounter more frequently.

Brian is over-burdened by financial problems and social isolation following the ending of a longstanding relationship. He is becoming increasingly depressed and is talking about suicide as a way out of his problems and to escape the emotional pain he is experiencing.

It is in circumstances like these that a counsellor experiences the choice between respect for the client's autonomy and acting to prevent self-destruction most acutely. In the United States a counsellor can be sued for failing to take prudent actions to prevent suicide or for over-reacting. In Britain, legal action is less likely although some counsellors have been asked to give evidence in a Coroner's Court following a client's suicide and have felt that their competence as a counsellor was being scrutinized by the court. Nonetheless, the problem facing the counsellor has been primarily an ethical rather than a legal one. The first step towards resolving the dilemma involves careful assessment of whether or not the client is capable of taking responsibility for his own decision and the degree of risk of suicide. The assessment procedure is not only to clarify the counsellor's responsibility but also has some therapeutic gains for the client because it enables him to review what may be an overwhelming single problem and break it down into its constituent parts, which may therefore become more manageable. From the counsellor's point of view, it is well known that it is extremely difficult to make infallible assessments of suicidal clients, indeed it is sometimes impossible to come to any definite conclusion. However, a carefully conducted assessment helps to establish that the counselling provided is of an adequate standard and that the counsellor is acting with a level of care commensurate with the potential seriousness of the situation.

Methods for conducting the assessment may vary between counsellors according to their background. Counsellors who prefer to avoid conventional psychiatric classifications may prefer the assessment process described by John Eldrid (1988) which is derived from his experience as a director of the Central London Branch of the Samaritans. Counsellors with a psychiatric training may prefer the assessment procedures advocated by Keith Hawton and Jose Catalan (1987). Although the procedures are described in different terminology they address the same tasks. These can be summarized as an assessment of:

1 suicidal intentions: strength of feelings about going on or ending it all; degree of planning and preparations already accomplished; exploration of client's intentions in any recent attempt at suicide;
2 clarification of current difficulties: exploration of nature of problems and duration, for example, loss of close relationship, job, finance, status, sexual or addiction difficulties, etc.;
3 psychological state: comparison between usual psychological state and present with particular regard to hopelessness, anxiety, guilt, obsessions, anger, dependency, inner isolation;
4 psychiatric history: previous history of mental illness and attempted suicide; and any evidence of current mental illness including depression;
5 resources for coping: the availability of support from social network of partner, friends, family, etc. and religious faith; previous coping strategies for problems.

Unless there is clear evidence to the contrary because, for example, the client is deluded or extremely confused, it is reasonable to conduct the assessment using methods which assume that the client is responsible for his or her own actions. Respect for his or her autonomy means that any consultations with others about the client during this assessment stage should either be done in ways which protect the client's personal identity or with the client's permission. This is important because the assessment of how to respond to a suicidal client is considerably helped by discussions with people with relevant experience. The availability of medical/ psychiatric treatment and the client's means of getting access to this may also need to be clarified by discussion with a doctor or mental health professional. This is not an alternative to the client making these enquiries for him or herself but acts as valuable background information for the counsellor's assessment of what options to put to the client. These consultations also have the effect of providing personal support for the counsellor and help to minimize the anxiety most counsellors experience in this situation. They also provide an opportunity for the counsellor to check their own assessment of the situation. At the end of the assessment procedure there are usually three possible conclusions.

First, the client is competent to take decisions for himself including whether to consent to counselling, other treatments and to take control of his living or dying. Counselling would continue by agreement with the client. In order to emphasize the client's responsibility some counsellors obtain written agreements from their clients that if they feel suicidal they will contact their own general practitioner and, if this is not possible, the Samaritans. Some counsellors obtain agreements from clients that they will not attempt suicide whilst the counselling is continuing. None of these agreements is enforceable against a suicidal client but they emphasize the client's responsibility for his or her own well-being and show that the counsellor has taken the suicidal intentions seriously.

Second, the mental state of the client may be such that there is real doubt that the client has the capacity to take responsibility for himself and there is a substantial risk of suicide. Ideally, the client will agree to seek a second opinion from a doctor, psychiatric nurse or approved social worker. If the client is unwilling to do this, then the counsellor may need to break confidentiality in order to obtain help. The *Code of Ethics and Practice for Counsellors* (BAC, 1990) contains the following guidance:

> B.4.4 Exceptional circumstances may arise which give the counsellor good grounds for believing that the client will cause serious physical harm to others or him/herself, or have harm caused to him/her. In such circumstances the client's consent to a change in the agreement about confidentiality should be sought whenever possible unless there are good

grounds for believing the client is no longer able to take responsibility for his/her own actions. Whenever possible, the decision to break confidentiality agreed between a counsellor and client should be made only after consultation with a counselling supervisor or an experienced counsellor.

B.4.5 Any breaking of confidentiality should be minimised both by restricting the information conveyed to that which is pertinent to the immediate situation and to those persons who can provide the help required by the client. The ethical considerations involve balancing between acting in the best interests of the client in ways which enable clients to resume taking responsibility for their actions, a very high priority for counsellors, and the counsellor's responsibilities to the wider community.

The decision about whether or not to break confidentiality in these circumstances is often very difficult. It is worth noting that the code does *not* require the counsellor to act but it is a matter for the counsellor's judgment. The counsellor has to balance the expressed wishes of the client against the knowledge of the client's capacity for taking responsibility for himself. The potential for the client being significantly helped by such a breach of confidence would also need to be taken into account.

Third, the client either lacks the maturity to understand the consequences of his actions or is so distressed or mentally disturbed that the client lacks the capacity to take responsibility for his or her own actions; there is a high risk of suicide; and there is the possibility of compulsory treatment under the Mental Health legislation. In these circumstances the counsellor would try to find a way of proceeding with the client's consent but these are probably the circumstances in which the client does need someone to take responsibility on his behalf on a temporary basis by the counsellor seeking the assistance of a doctor or approved social worker.

As a general rule the best practice with regard to suicidal clients works in ways which respect the client's autonomy and right to choose until there are substantial grounds for doubting a client's capacity to take responsibility for himself; and there is a serious risk of suicide and there is the possibility of an alternative way of intervening. In these exceptional circumstances a counsellor may intervene to prevent the client's self-destruction.

References

Eldrid, John (1988) *Caring for the Suicidal*. London: Constable.

Hawton, Keith and Catalan, Jose (1987) *Attempted Suicide – A Practical Guide to its Nature and Management* (2nd edn). Oxford: Oxford University Press.

Laing, R.D. (1967) *The Politics of Experience*. Harmondsworth: Penguin.

Szasz, Thomas S. (1986) 'The case against suicide prevention', *American Psychology*, 41(7): 806–12.

PART SIX

PROFESSIONAL ISSUES

24a Psychology and counselling

Does being a psychologist help a counsellor in his or her work?

Michael Carroll

It is hard to imagine that spending at least three years studying psychology would not be of benefit to the counsellor. After all, most psychology courses include modules on personality, developmental stages of life through which individuals travel, social aspects of living, cognition and how people learn. Already, these studies provide a formidable body of knowledge to help those working with individuals or groups. Applied areas of psychology are also presented to students, for example, understanding and managing stress, models of intervention and occupational life. The amount of information available from psychological study is immense, providing valuable 'working knowledge' for the counsellor.

But maybe that is answering the question too lightly. Three years studying 'anything' brings with it mind-sets, ways of thinking, prejudices that can be detrimental when transferred into or onto another profession. Conversions can all too readily result in dogmatic, restricted ways of thinking and behaving, rather than freedom, openness and integration. Could being a psychologist be a disadvantage to being a counsellor? Some people think so. Psychologists, they say, are trained, probably too well trained, in specific ways of thinking about people, and particularly in ways of researching, to be of any major help to counsellors. They are too given to testing, making mechanical formulations, and treating persons as if they were animals only, to enter the live world of interacting with individuals. And anyway, some people comment, counselling is an art and psychology a science, and what psychologists do is try to make counselling into a science, and destroy it.

On the other hand, counselling psychology has been a profession in the USA for quite some time. Whiteley (1984) has traced its history from 1908 to 1983 through seven periods, outlining its beginnings from 'numerous and diverse initial roots' to its establishment as a recognized profession in the 1950s. Presumably, and by definition, counselling psychologists are psychologists who are counsellors. In the USA there are PhD programmes in counselling psychology and in Britain a number of programmes at Masters level in counselling psychology, many of which are taught in departments of psychology. Counselling and psychology have been married for some time now, even though reservations are expressed about the advisability of that union.

So perhaps a better answer to the question of whether or not being a psychologist helps a counsellor in his or her work, is: it depends. It depends on the psychologist and how he or she is able to use their knowledge, and it depends on the psychology and how open it is to dialogue and conversation and integration.

I will put forward some ways in which I think psychology could be of benefit to the counsellor. First of all psychology can provide information from an array of areas to enlighten the counsellor. I teach a course on 'Personality Theory and Counselling' in which themes from the psychology of personality are reviewed and applied to counselling. A recent book by Cramer (1991) entitled *Personality and Psychotherapy* also attempts to combine these two concepts. Looking at the underlying concept of the person behind counselling models helps articulate the different understandings of the person, and how and why counselling models differ. It also helps counsellors to identify their own implicit 'personality theory' and test how congruent they are in what they believe and in what they practise. Other interesting 'personality themes' revolve around the role of the unconscious in the life of the person; and what difference does it make whether we start from the notion of the healthy or the unhealthy personality? What does the personality of the counsellor him- or herself contribute to counselling? Through the latter question, counsellors can begin to look at why people choose to become counsellors (has it anything to do with their personality?), and trainees can spend some time exploring their own motivation. If the personality of the counsellor has such an impact on effectiveness of counselling (McConnaughy, 1987), then understanding one's own personality can be invaluable to the counsellor.

More and more counselling programmes realize the value of their students having some insights into the developmental stages of life and the tasks faced by individuals as they grow older. Developmental psychology has a lot to offer in this field and a number of authors have combined counselling and developmental psychology (Ivey, 1986; Woolfe and Sugarman, 1989; Thomas, 1990). Helping individuals successfully negotiate the pathways through life takes up a major part of counselling. For those working with adolescents it helps enormously to understand some of the issues they are facing and how these might be expressed in their lives. Developmental psychology has shown that the focus of life in teenage years is on the body, and the adolescent's feeling that their inward thoughts are expressed physically is helpful when working with them. It helps me, as a counsellor, adapt my approach. Knowing some of their reserve about the adult world, and realizing they are suspicious of adults who are warm and friendly on their first contact (after all teenagers are a marketable age group to be enticed into parting with their money – by adults, mostly) I am more formal at the beginning of our sessions. I use less eye contact with teenagers, especially those who are disturbed or aggressive. My information from psychology, and indeed my subsequent experience, has taught me that they are extremely self-conscious, and very anxious lest the counsellor understands them better than they understand themselves. This is anxiety-provoking for anyone, and exaggerated in adolescence. Similar insights about other stages of life can contribute to the way counsellors work with clients.

There are other areas of information provided by psychology that are useful to the counsellor. Social psychology reminds us that the contexts in which individuals live and the influence that systems have on individuals are crucial in working with people (Egan and Cowan, 1979). Counsellors have often been criticized for seeing problems as emanating solely from within the person and for not recognizing the full extent of how individuals are products of the systems in which they live. Social psychology reminds the counsellor of this with its information and research on interpersonal life, family and social life, and influences from the wider community.

Besides informing, psychology can challenge counsellors to research their work. It is very easy within counselling to assume that our counselling orientation is the only way to work and that if clients are not helped then, automatically, assume it is the client's fault. We need to research counselling if for no other reason than to assure our clients that they are getting the best service possible. Psychologists are no longer as narrow in the methods they use for research (Heppner, Kivlighan and Wampold, 1992), and are devising interesting methodologies to understand and test the various elements in the counselling process.

In summary, psychology can help the counsellor in a number of ways. It provides helpful information from a variety of psychological sources. That information can be 'working knowledge' through which the counsellor sifts the client and their world to help assess what is happening and understand some of the dynamics involved. It also influences counselling interventions, for example, how a counsellor and client might formulate a treatment plan, and/or work out a new learning strategy for the client. Techniques and strategies used to help the client gain insight or facilitate change can emerge from psychological information, as in the example above with teenagers.

Furthermore, psychology challenges counselling to research its effectiveness. It can provide personality tests to enable the counsellor to back up their own assessment of clients with objective means. For a fuller account of the relationship between psychology and counselling see Carroll and Pickard (in press). However, if all this leaves you unconvinced that psychology can (but need not necessarily) be a positive influence, then one further interesting piece of information might swing the balance. In a recent research project (Sharpley and Ridgway, 1991) in Australia, the authors looked at the difference in counselling skills training between trainees with a psychology background (undergraduate degree in psychology) and those without such a degree. Using 'a five-week training programme based upon micro-skills and a systematic model' (1991: 298) they trained psychology graduates and non-psychology trainees in counselling skills. The results, in their view, were quite conclusive, 'Trainees with backgrounds in psychology were significantly superior to trainees without a similar background' (1991: 298). My understanding of this conclusion is that it is more helpful to the counsellor to have a psychology background than not to have one from the perspective of skills training, and that immediately after training psychology graduates are more effective than non-psychology graduates.

Conclusion

Even though some contend that being a psychologist is harmful to counselling work, it seems to me that psychology provides a lot of useful aids to the counsellor: information, interventions, assessment procedures and research methods that can help evaluate the effectiveness of counselling. However, it is how these are used, as well as the aids themselves, that will determine whether or not the influence is positive.

References

Carroll, M. and Pickard, E. (in press) 'Psychology and counselling', in B. Thorne and W. Dryden (eds), *Counselling: Interdisciplinary Perspectives*. Buckingham: Open University Press.

Cramer, D. (1991) *Personality and Psychotherapy: Theory, Practice and Research*. Buckingham: Open University Press.

Egan, G. and Cowan, M. (1979) *People in Systems*. Monterey, CA: Brooks/Cole.

Heppner, P.P., Kivlighan, D.M. and Wampold, B. (1992) *Research Design in Counseling*. Pacific Grove, CA: Brooks/Cole.

Ivey, A. (1986) *Developmental Theory*. London: Jossey-Bass.

McConnaughy, E.A. (1987) 'The person of the therapist in psychotherapeutic practice', *Psychotherapy*, 24(3): 303–14.

Sharpley, C.F. and Ridgway, I.R. (1991) 'The relevance of previous knowledge of psychology to training in basic counselling skills', *British Journal of Guidance and Counselling*, 19(3): 298–306.

Thomas, R.M. (1990) *Counselling and Life-Span Development*. London: Sage.

Whiteley, J.M. (1984) 'A historical perspective on the development of counseling psychology as a profession', pp. 3–55 in S. Brown and R. Lent (eds), *The Handbook of Counseling Psychology*. New York: Wiley.

Woolfe, R. and Sugarman, L. (1989) 'Counselling and the life cycle', in W. Dryden, D. Charles-Edwards and R. Woolfe (eds), *Handbook of Counselling in Britain*. London: Routledge.

24b   Psychology and counselling

Does being a psychologist help a counsellor in his or her work?

Emmy van Deurzen-Smith

Why should being a psychologist help a counsellor in his or her work? Does this question assume that psychology and counselling are of the same order? Is it true then that being a psychologist is about understanding people, not just as statistics or objects, but as they are really in their everyday struggles? What is it that psychology has to offer to counsellors? Psychology, defined as the scientific study of the mind, unfortunately remains a very limited and restricted field at present. Much of it is not directly relevant to counselling.

Why psychology?

To be sure, the acquisition of carefully selected psychological knowledge and expertise will not go amiss when training to become a counsellor, but nor would the study of social work, political or educational science, human history, biology, sociology, anthropology, philosophy or medicine. There are many disciplines that are pertinent to the counsellor's work and psychology is just one of them. But it would be a grave error to make psychology and counselling out to be the most compatible of all these possible partnerships. Doing so would lead to an unnecessary psychologizing of the profession of counselling, something that I believe to be as undesirable as medicalization of counselling.

Of course there will always be room for medical counselling in relation to medical problems that need to be aired and discussed together with a patient. In the same way there will always be room for psychological counselling, when clients are specifically dealing with characterological or personality problems. In the context of a psychological testing situation it would be highly desirable for the counselling or clinical psychologist to be available for some counselling sessions to help the client work through the issues highlighted.

Why not psychology?

In other words counselling and psychology are in principle complementary and compatible: the counsellor might also be a psychologist and the psychologist could be a counsellor. Being a psychologist might, in some specific situation, enhance one's counselling work, but there is no reason to assume that all counselling is improved if the counsellor is a trained psychologist. One could imagine a future situation where psychology would have become a more broadly based investigation of all that our clients are preoccupied with, making it a conceivable proposition that being a psychologist would help counsellors in their work. This is not, however, the present situation.

What kind of counselling do we want?

In order to get a clear picture of the relationship between counselling and psychology we really need to define the notion of 'counselling'. If we accept the definition recently developed by the Lead Body for Advice, Guidance and Counselling we will soon see that counselling is a great deal broader than it would become if counsellors were psychologists first.

The definition states that

> counselling is an activity freely entered into by the person seeking help, it offers the opportunity to identify things for the clients themselves that are troubling or perplexing. It is clearly and explicitly contracted, and the boundaries of the relationship identified. The activity itself is designed to help self-exploration and understanding. The process should help to identify thoughts, emotions and behaviours that, once assessed, may offer the client opportunities for a greater sense of personal resources and self determined change. (Russell, Dexter and Bond, 1992)

Reversal of the question

Faced with such a definition it may well be that we need to reverse the entire question. The answer may become a great deal more interesting if we ask ourselves whether the opposite might be true: whether there might be some reason to conclude that counselling could be impeded and hindered if the counsellor were a psychologist.

My personal answer is that this might be the case as psychology and counselling are quite distinct professions. It is perfectly feasible for one person to be trained in both, but this requires a particular flexibility on the part of the professional, in the same way in which it requires a particular flexibility for someone to be both a doctor and a counsellor. On the whole I believe that such flexibility is a good thing, adding a new dimension to the practice of both professions. I think that psychologists are improved as professionals by training in counselling and by having the experience of doing counselling work. Equally I think that counsellors' work could improve by a closer study of psychology. Cross-fertilization and inter-disciplinary work add breadth and strength and this inevitably enhances professional work.

Further questions

Clearly some more poignant questions are imbedded in the debate, which it might be interesting to address briefly. These are:

1 Should counsellors be required to be psychologists?
2 Should a psychology background be considered sufficient training to become a counsellor?
3 Is psychology the most important knowledge base for the practice of counselling?

Although I would easily concede that psychology and counselling have much to offer each other, it would be quite a different matter to make it a requirement for counsellors to also be psychologists. A diet of pure psychology would be likely to alienate counsellors from the human dimension of their profession, for while psychology prides itself in its emphasis on objectivity, counselling is about understanding people in the context of their human predicament.

Counselling in this sense is as much about anthropology and sociology as it is about psychology. In addition, counselling concerns itself with questions of meaning and being as well as with the person and in this sense it is philosophy or even ontology that are relevant. A pure diet of psychology would therefore be an absurd constraint for the counsellor. It would be a diet that would have to be seriously supplemented with other ingredients if the psychologist were to turn to counselling, if a one-sided and biased intervention is to be avoided.

Irrelevance of the original question

In some ways it is remarkable that we should be asking the initial question at all. We could with nearly as much justification ask whether being a vicar, a priest or a rabbi would help a counsellor in his or her work. Or, for that matter, we could ask whether being a man or a woman helps, or whether being married, single or

divorced, or having children or having a particular sexual orientation would help. All of these obviously have some bearing upon
the sort of counsellor a person will be, in the same way in which
being a psychologist will also have a certain bearing on the way in
which one counsels. What should be clear is that such issues are
merely a matter of preference, of specific extras that a counsellor
can bring to the job. They can in no way be treated as prescriptive
requirements and the extent to which they help or hinder the
professional depends largely on what he or she does with this
particular given.

The real issue

At the same time, by dismissing psychology as a necessary, sufficient or even desirable condition for doing counselling, we are in
danger of throwing the baby out with the bath-water. Indeed, by
noting that psychology as a discipline is not the most useful
backdrop to the profession of counselling at present, we invite the
question of what would be the most useful or helpful background
for a counsellor. This is a question well worth asking and exploring. When a new profession is born there is the opportunity to
create a whole new approach to training and education, but the
temptation is to force it to conform with existing professions and
their training and education.

Looking back to the birth of psychoanalysis, which provides a
close enough parallel, it is worth noting how Freud spoke about
the ideal training for the analyst. He said:

> analytic instruction would include branches of knowledge which are
> remote from medicine and which the doctor does not come across in his
> practice: the history of civilization, mythology, the psychology of
> religion and the science of literature. Unless he is well at home in these
> subjects, an analyst can make nothing of a large amount of his material.
> By way of compensation, the great mass of what is taught in medical
> schools is of no use to him for his purposes. (Freud, 1926: 246)

In the same way a substantial amount of what psychologists are
taught in their studies, especially in terms of testing and statistical
analysis, is irrelevant to the counsellor. In addition, much that a
psychologist would be ignorant of is of great importance for the
profession of counselling.

What is a helpful background for the counsellor?

The person who is going to counsel others in relation to everything
that concerns them, must be educated and trained in the broadest

possible range of subjects that are relevant. But, in my opinion, before this it is important for the counsellor to be a mature and well-balanced person. It is crucial that he or she has actually lived life intensely, having encountered many obstacles and having tackled them successfully. It is equally important that the counsellor has been exposed to many different aspects of life, has lived in different contexts, cultures and circumstances, so that his or her viewpoint is wide enough and varied enough to encompass most of the client's frustrations and questions.

As we cannot gain first-hand experience of much of life, it is all the more imperative that we should at least gain second-hand experience. Literature, I would argue, is in this sense a better teacher than psychology. For by the process of reading about other people, we identify directly with them and gain a kind of insight into their struggles. Yes, I would consider that travel, literature, the overcoming of personal predicaments and having to survive alien conditions are all more likely to enhance the counsellor's work then being a psychologist would.

In terms of formal study, I would rank psychology lower than philosophy, because philosophy (especially classical, continental or non-Western philosophy) enquires into the human condition and asks precisely the sort of questions that people who seek out counsellors puzzle over. Psychology, to my mind, is only a small aspect of this sort of study and, in addition, tends to provide answers instead of being sensitive to the need to question. It fails to make room for mystery, doubt, faith, paradox and many other typically human experiences. In fairness, there is also much in philosophy that is not directly relevant to counsellors.

Might being a psychologist hinder the counsellor's work?

Finally, it may be valuable to consider the other side of the coin of the question asked, namely 'Might being a psychologist hinder a counsellor in his or her work?' Here I shall speak from personal experience instead of arguing the case. I became a psychologist after I had already been a counsellor for a number of years. As such, I was able to be both selective in what I took from psychology and aware of the possible damaging impact of psychological studies for the practice of counselling and psychotherapy. I have encountered only too many psychologists whose attitude would be totally contrary to that needed from a counsellor. Psychologists all too often look for certainty, for facts and data that can provide an unswerving direction. It is in my view of the utmost importance that counsellors should not have this need for certainty or this belief in unwavering scientific truths. While the openness of the true scientific spirit would be an asset to the counsellor, the sad fact is that much of science is a search for dogma. But then again some non-scientific, non-psychologist counsellors are also stuck in boxed-in positions and fixed convictions. All too many counsellors are willing to blindly duplicate interventions that are based on simplistic formulae. Often these are based on little more than the quixotic prescriptions of a particular author, who happens to be in fashion.

Somehow, counselling is in need of a discipline that will enable counsellors to accept that reality can not be fastened to a blueprint of life that can be endlessly reproduced. It needs a background method and specialized study that will allow for life's varying and diverse reality. To have the ability to contain the paradoxes that life exposes us to without losing the sense of perspective requires something very different than what is required from the mind of the psychologist. But it may also require a somewhat greater rigour than is current in existing counselling training.

Reformulating the question

This leads to a reformulation of the original question in a different manner. For now we can begin to wonder how the field of counselling might transform our view of psychology. 'Would being a counsellor enhance one's work as a psychologist?', we could ask. And the answer would be: 'Yes, if the counsellor had been trained so as to increase his or her human perspective and decrease her or his prejudice.' Yes, in that case, I believe that psychology would gain much from counselling.

Because of this, it seems to me that the rapidly developing branch of counselling psychology is a tremendous step forward for psychology, precisely in that it proposes a marriage of the knowledge and research base of psychology and the praxis of counselling. Handled creatively such a marriage can become a most productive and fertile occasion for both psychologists and counsellors. But recognizing the potential of such a coming together of two disciplines should by no means make us give in to the temptation to reduce all counselling to counselling psychology and profess that counselling should really find its proper and ultimate base in psychology.

Perhaps counselling would be better off turning to cognitive science for its knowledge base. This is itself a developing cross-disciplinary venture between philosophy, psychology, computer science and linguistics. Of course phenomenology or ethnomethodology also have a lot to offer to the developing speciality of counselling. And, yes, I believe that counselling would improve with a more efficient and comprehensive charting of the terrain of human experience. But in order to find the appropriate knowledge base I think it would do well to go a little further afield than to mainstream establishment psychology.

Whether counselling has as much to gain from psychology as psychology might have to gain from counselling, I seriously doubt.

References

Freud, S. (1926) 'The question of lay-analysis', *Complete Works of Sigmund Freud*, Vol. 20. London: Hogarth Press.

Russell, J., Dexter, G. and Bond, T. (1992) *A Report on Differentiation between Advice, Guidance, Befriending, Counselling Skills and Counselling*. London: Department of Employment.

25 Research and practice

As students of counselling we are constantly urged to read the research literature on counselling on the basis that it will help us to become more effective practitioners. However, many of us complain that even after reading numerous research studies on the process and outcome of counselling, we find little to inform our counselling practice. What are we missing?

Michael Barkham

Understanding the relationship between research and practice

The complaint that counselling (and psychotherapy) research literature does not inform practice is both an old and, unfortunately, a consistent one. In large part, it derives from researchers and practitioners asking different questions and focusing on different issues, with researchers tending to address academic questions which do not necessarily appear to have sufficient immediacy for practitioners. Beyond that, there are two viewpoints which can be taken about the relationship between research and practice. One is that research should *precede* and thereby directly influence counselling practice: that is, researchers 'discover' aspects of counselling which, when applied, fundamentally alter (or at least modify) practice. This equates counselling research with medical research, where vasts sums of money are invested in long-term trials of drugs or other procedures which are then adopted by the profession. The assumption that this position should also hold for counselling (as well as psychotherapy) generates misunderstanding and false expectations. Contrary to the role of research in medicine, research in counselling (and the cognate disciplines of psychotherapy and clinical psychology) has invariably *followed* practice. This has occurred for the simple reason that the skills of the counsellor do not rely on the application of external agents (that is, drugs or highly sophisticated equipment). Each counsellor can experiment and test out their own procedures, thus enabling them to innovate and test out 'new' approaches within everyday practice. It is hardly surprising then that research lags behind such practice. Accordingly, an alternative view of the relation between research and practice is one of providing *confirmation* of counselling 'wisdom' and increasing our *understanding* of, for example, the mechanisms of change (that is, how change occurs). Additionally, it should not be forgotten that research often produces non-significant findings which, although equally important, appear less impressive both to practitioners and research journals alike. Thus a considerable amount of research effort fails to influence practice. Similarly, there are no definitive studies in counselling or psychotherapy (Barkham and Shapiro, 1992). Rather, the available knowledge base has to be built upon a series of studies, which necessarily takes time. However, these points notwithstanding, there is a body of research findings which has accrued and which does have a bearing upon counselling practice. This piece presents a selection of findings grouped under two headings: first, research on the structure and outcome of a service delivery system, and second, research on the counselling process.

The structure and outcome of a counselling service delivery system

It has long been held, albeit implicitly, that the more counselling clients receive, the more they will improve. Recent research has corroborated this view but has also provided a very powerful caveat. Howard et al. (1986) found that while a greater percentage of clients improved the longer they remained in therapy, there were diminishing returns. Major gains tended to be achieved during the initial eight to twelve sessions and certainly by twenty-six sessions, after which the number of clients showing measurable improvement reduced markedly. However, clients presenting with differing constellations of problems showed different response rates and research suggests that such clients require long-term counselling (Shapiro et al., 1992). The implication for practice is that for clients presenting with, for example, depression, briefer forms of counselling may be cost-effective. For example, contracts of eight or twelve sessions might be appropriate, while for clients presenting with lower-severity problems there is interest in adopting and evaluating the 'two-plus-one' model under certain selected conditions (Barkham and Shapiro, 1990). However, there is current concern about the possibility of potentially high relapse rates from administering short-term interventions. A related finding which bears upon the issue of service delivery is whether to offer open-ended or time-limited contracts. Research evidence suggests that the effectiveness of counselling and therapy is broadly equivalent under both conditions (see Orlinsky and Howard, 1986). However, it needs to be remembered that time-limited contracts can comprise more sessions than open-ended contracts, hence increasing the impact of time-limited contracts.

In terms of using either an individual or group approach, Orlinsky and Howard (1986) found the weight of evidence from research studies showed no significant difference between individual and group approaches, although Robinson et al.'s (1990) review suggested a slight but non-significant advantage to an individual approach. However, there is a suggestion that the issue is a more complex one. For example, Piper et al. (1984) compared four types of approaches: long-term group, short-term group, long-term individual and short-term individual. They found short-term individual and long-term group therapies to be most effective and, equally important, they argued that these two approaches were also the most cost-effective. However, regardless of approaches, Orlinsky and Howard (1986) reported that one of the best predictors of good outcome is whether or not clients have received some prior induction into the counselling/therapy process. Of thirty-four findings, twenty-one showed significantly better outcomes for clients who received some form of role preparation. Overall, in terms of structuring a counselling service, the above findings provide support for considering offering brief, time-limited counselling and for providing clients with some form of role preparation. However, clients presenting with more severe problems clearly require more counselling, and there is a suggestion that a long-term group approach may be worth considering.

In terms of the 'content' of the therapy offered, research has, with the exception of a single study (Prioleau et al., 1983), reported that active treatments do better than placebo treatments which, in turn, do better than no-treatment conditions (Lambert et al., 1986). This simple but consistent finding has the implication that while placebo treatments are more beneficial than, for example, being placed on a waiting list, clients will in general show greater benefit from receiving a form of counselling which is based on some theoretical model (for example, cognitive-behavioural, psychodynamic, etc.). Although the size of the difference is relatively small, it does raise the question as to whether it is ethical for counsellors to offer clients any form of intervention which could be described as a placebo.

Within active models of counselling, one question which has dominated research and which has also been of major interest to practitioners concerns the comparative effectiveness of contrasting counselling orientations. However, research studies investigating potential differences between contrasting active orientations have continually reported no major differences: contrasting approaches (usually psychodynamic versus cognitive-behavioural) are *broadly* equivalent in their effectiveness (for example, Elkin et al., 1989). In other words, there is *generally* little difference between the differing theoretical approaches used by counsellors. Where there is a reported advantage (to any particular orientation), the size of the advantage tends to be very small. Accordingly, research findings suggest there is no ethical dilemma in adopting one theoretical orientation over another. A corollary of this position, and a major issue for practitioners, is that this provides the basis for moving towards more integrative models of counselling and therapy. As such, research findings have provided a powerful ethical defence for (a) selecting a preferred counselling approach and (b) for adopting an integrative approach. However, not all clients will benefit equally from one particular approach.

There is a literature suggesting certain specific treatments for specific problems, although these tend to be more in the area of psychophysiological problems (for example, headaches). Reviews attempting to test whether neurotic, phobic and emotional problems respond differentially to specific interventions have been inconclusive (for example, Shapiro, 1985). Whatever the counselling orientation or presenting problem, it needs to be remembered that some clients deteriorate through counselling. However, a research design does not exist which could adequately test the hypothesis that such deterioration would have been greater had they not received counselling. Whatever counselling orientation is adopted, however, there is a small but consistent pattern of findings in the literature (see Orlinsky and Howard, 1986) suggesting a *negative* association between delay in implementing counselling and outcome: that is, clients forced to wait tend to have poorer outcomes. Given that these findings are predictive of negative outcomes, they are especially important in informing how a service can best be utilized. Overall, the above findings suggest active treatment approaches should be adopted but at present there appears to be little to help practitioners select the actual counselling orientation used, except that the sooner it is offered the better.

The counselling process

For simplicity of presentation, research findings reported here will be grouped in two sections: first, those research findings addressing *specific* factors (for example, types of verbal interventions) and, second, those addressing *common* factors (for example, the client–

counsellor relationship). In terms of specific factors, Orlinsky and Howard's (1986) review of research findings focusing on the range of verbal interventions made in counselling drew a number of conclusions. In relation to the effects of interpretation, exactly one-half of the available findings showed this form of intervention to have a significantly positive effect on outcome, suggesting a rather equivocal association. By contrast, although fewer studies have been carried out, research findings relating to 'confrontations' (which aim to provide the client with insight *and* a directly meaningful experience but contain no element of hostility) showed total consistency in being significantly and positively related with client outcome. In terms of the findings addressing the impact of 'reflections', Orlinsky and Howard concluded: 'Reflection seems to be neither helpful nor harmful in itself, and thus compares poorly with techniques that do have some therapeutic potency' (1986: 330). Similarly, in terms of 'support', three-quarters of findings showed no association between offered support and client outcome. While considerable research effort has been spent on interventions, surprisingly little research has focused on the skilfulness of the counsellor. What research has been carried out has consistently shown skilfulness to be significantly associated with client outcome. Research in this area is critical for the profession as well as a challenge for participating counsellors. Indeed, it may be one aspect of counselling practice which will reveal large individual differences between various groups of counsellors and, if so, will have considerable implications both for training and practice.

In terms of common factors, there are interesting findings relating to the impact of placebo treatments. For example, there is evidence that clients may be able to use 'chats' just as therapeutically as a specific therapeutic intervention (Burton et al., 1991). One explanation for such a finding may be the potency of the therapeutic relationship between client and counsellor. Current work in this area has developed from earlier research work on the 'facilitative conditions' but is not synonymous with it. Lambert (1992) summarizes ten studies investigating the role of the therapeutic alliance in client outcome. One study reported no association while the other nine reported positive associations. On average, the nine studies suggested that 25 per cent of outcome variance could be accounted for by the status of the therapeutic relationship, although there was a considerable range across the studies. Thus, while research findings are not unanimous in finding a positive relationship between therapeutic alliance and outcome, findings do suggest two points. First, that on average, around one-quarter of a client's outcome can be accounted for by the state of the therapeutic relationship between client and counsellor and, second, that the range for this association is considerable: for some clients it is important while for others it is less so.

Looking at the above findings on specific and common factors, the available research would appear to suggest that the skills comprising the common factors should not be viewed as anything other than central and critical within training and practice. Indeed, Lambert (1992) suggests that research indicates common factors to account for upwards of 30 per cent of outcome variance while specific factors account for approximately half this amount. However, while many verbal interventions appear to be neither harmful nor specifically helpful, there is a developing literature on the value of certain specific techniques (for example, confrontations). Implications for practice are that such specific interventions may be particularly effective in facilitating client change but the exact interrelationship between specific and common factors requires considerable further research before clear guidelines for practice could be made with confidence (for example, Jones et al., 1988).

Conclusion

In absolute terms, the above selection of findings suggests that research in counselling and its cognate disciplines has informed various aspects of practice, although more so in the area of outcome than process. In relative terms, however, it is likely that practitioners will continue to be disappointed with the yield of counselling and psychotherapy research given the emphasis placed upon it in, for example, training programmes. While there are considerable conceptual and methodological problems in any research endeavour, particularly when linking process findings with outcome (see Stiles and Shapiro, 1989), much of the disappointment can be attributed to the poor quality of many research studies, in particular, the design and methodology employed. Greater emphasis should be placed on carrying out high quality research which is seen as responsive to the needs of counselling practice. Equally, intense counselling observation by practitioners can feed into and inform counselling theory, which can in turn be tested empirically through more formal research procedures. For those readers actively interested in research findings, the following are suggested. A useful text for the future will be the forthcoming fourth edition of the *Handbook of Psychotherapy and Behavior Change* (edited by Garfield and Bergin); key counselling research journals include *Psychotherapy Research, Journal of Counseling Psychology* and *Counselling Psychology Quarterly*; while active research-based meetings are held by the UK chapter of the Society for Psychotherapy Research.

References

Barkham, M. and Shapiro, D.A. (1990) 'Brief psychotherapeutic interventions for job-related distress: a pilot study of prescriptive and exploratory therapy', *Counselling Psychology Quarterly*, 3: 133–47.

Barkham, M. and Shapiro D.A. (1992) 'Problems of methodology in studies of psychotherapy: response', in W. Dryden and C. Feltham (eds), *Psychotherapy and its Discontents*. Buckingham: Open University Press.

Burton, M.V., Parker, R.W. and Wollner, J.M. (1991) 'The psychotherapeutic value of a "chat": a verbal response modes study of a placebo attention control with breast cancer patients', *Psychotherapy Research*, 1: 39–61.

Elkin, I., Shea, M.T., Watkins, J.T., Imber, S.D., Sotsky, S.M., Collins, J.F., Glass, D.R., Pilkonis, P.A., Leber, W.R., Docherty, J.P., Fiester, S.J. and Parloff, M.B. (1989) 'National Institute of Mental Health Treatment of Depression Collaborative Research Program: general effectiveness of treatments', *Archives of General Psychiatry*, 46: 971–82.

Howard, K.I., Kopta, S.M., Krause, M.S. and Orlinsky, D.E. (1986) 'The dose–effect relationship in psychotherapy', *American Psychologist*, 41: 159–64.

Jones, E.E., Cumming, J.D. and Horowitz, M.J. (1988) 'Another look at the nonspecific hypothesis of therapeutic effectiveness', *Journal of Consulting and Clinical Psychology*, 56: 48–55.

Lambert, M.J. (1992) 'Psychotherapy outcome research: implications for integrative and eclectic therapists', in J.C. Norcross and M.R. Goldfried (eds), *Handbook of Psychotherapy Integration*. New York: Basic Books.

Lambert, M.J., Shapiro, D.A. and Bergin, A.E. (1986) 'The effectiveness of psychotherapy', in S.L. Garfield and A.E. Bergin (eds), *Handbook of Psychotherapy and Behavior Change* (3rd edn). New York: John Wiley & Sons.

Orlinsky, D.E. and Howard, K.I. (1986) 'Process and outcome in psychotherapy', in S.L. Garfield and A.E. Bergin (eds), *Handbook of Psychotherapy and Behavior Change* (3rd edn). New York: John Wiley & Sons.

Piper, W.E., Debbane, E.G., Bienvenu, J.P. and Garant, J. (1984) 'A comparative study of four forms of psychotherapy', *Journal of Consulting and Clinical Psychology*, 52: 268–79.

Prioleau, L., Murdock, M. and Brody, N. (1983) 'An analysis of psychotherapy versus placebo studies', *Behavioral and Brain Sciences*, 6: 275–310.

Robinson, L.A., Berman, J.S. and Neimeyer, R.A. (1990) 'Psychotherapy for the treatment of depression: a comparative review of controlled outcome research', *Psychological Bulletin*, 108: 30–49.

Shapiro, D.A. (1985) 'Recent applications of meta-analysis in clinical research', *Clinical Psychology Review*, 5: 13–34.

Shapiro, D.A., Barkham, M., Hardy, G.E., Rees, A., Reynolds, S. and Startup, M. (1992) 'Prescriptive vs. exploratory psychotherapy for depression: outcomes of the Second Sheffield Psychotherapy Project', Paper presented at the International Meeting of the Society for Psychotherapy Research, Berkeley, California.

Stiles, W.B. and Shapiro, D.A. (1989) 'Abuse of the drug metaphor in psychotherapy process–outcome research', *Clinical Psychology Review*, 9: 521–43.

26 Evaluating counselling: guidelines for practice

How can counsellors best evaluate their work without being skilled in statistical methods or research design?

Michael Barkham

Many counsellors are interested in evaluating their work but are daunted by the prospect of having to use sophisticated designs and/or complex statistics. The purpose of this chapter is to present some general strategies and approaches in carrying out counselling evaluation. While the incentive for many counsellors to carry out evaluation will be a reflection of 'good practice' and of their ongoing professional development, there are increasing external pressures for health professionals to demonstrate the effectiveness of service delivery systems to a range of 'stakeholders': for example, managers and budget-holders, as well as to clients themselves. Although it might appear that the end result would be the same, the particular reason for evaluating counselling may well determine the kind of data which will be collected as well as how it is presented (Barkham, 1992). Indeed, it is important to be aware of the various 'stakeholders' in any counselling service. This is particularly true when drawing a distinction between audit and evaluation. For example, a service audit aims to establish *who* uses a service and how resources are allocated, while a quality assurance method focuses on *how* a service is delivered and involves the setting and monitoring of standards for performance. In contrast to audit, evaluation aims to address questions about the general *effectiveness* of counselling. Parry (1992) presents a useful résumé of the issues involved in audit and evaluation. Issues relating to both audit and evaluation are addressed in this chapter.

Service audit and quality assurance

Although there are multiple terms used in the area of service evaluation, it is useful to highlight two in particular: service audit and quality assurance. Service audit requires the collection of data on who is using the service and is a self-monitoring exercise (that is, it does not require external consultants). The data set will comprise information on the referral channels used by clients, demographics of clients and some taxonomy of the initial presenting issues. It may also include information on the orientation and duration of counselling. Information arising from a quality assurance exercise can lead to the monitoring, via a quality circle, of practical issues such as how long clients have to wait before being allocated to counselling and whether clients are seen promptly at the allocated time. With more resources, it is possible to monitor the quality of service offered through regular peer group supervision meetings. The quality of counselling offered could also be monitored through the use of audio-taped sessions. In this instance, the focus is directly on the quality of the within-session counselling which is being offered.

Evaluating counselling services

Maxwell (1984) has identified six dimensions which can be measured and therefore used in evaluating a counselling service: (1) relevance/appropriateness, (2) equity, (3) accessibility, (4) acceptability, (5) effectiveness and (6) efficiency. The first four of these are relatively self-explanatory. *Relevance/appropriateness* asks whether the service is matching the needs of the clients as determined by an initial assessment, while *equity* asks whether any subgroup of clients is being excluded from the service. *Accessibility* issues are addressed by a combination of geography and length of waiting lists, while *acceptability* addresses issues of whether clients are satisfied with the quality of service provided. Client satisfaction surveys are often advocated. On the face of it, this appears sensible as it provides a means for clients to feed back their views about the service they have received. However, the majority of clients tend to give relatively high scores for the services they have received, thereby making the exercise less informative than might have been expected. As Parry (1992) suggests, it may be better to ask clients explicitly for their dissatisfaction with the service. Alternatively, it may be more useful to obtain qualitative comments from clients (see below). The major focus for the remainder of this chapter will be on the last two dimensions: *effectiveness* and *efficiency*. Questions of effectiveness and efficiency are paramount and, while each dimension stands alone, they are highly interrelated. A practice can be effective in terms of satisfactory outcomes and yet result in high costs and a slow service. Equally, a service can be efficient in responding to clients very quickly and yet be ineffective in leading to client change. Recognizing the importance of both dimensions, the notion of *cost-effectiveness* may be the most useful to adopt whereby practitioners are aiming to achieve a given outcome at the lowest cost.

Quantitative evaluation of outcomes

More often than not, the most basic issue in evaluation is some variant of the question 'Has this client improved?' Any response to this question assumes a minimum data set comprising data at two time points: pre- and post-counselling. However, while adopting this simple design is clearly better than having no evaluation at all, it is easy to see a number of shortcomings. First, taking measures at two potentially distant points in time (that is, pre- and post-counselling) tells us nothing about what is happening in the time in between these two points. This is what is sometimes referred to as the 'process of outcome'. Second, measures taken at any one point in time do not provide particularly stable data. For example, we might have greater confidence in the distress reported by a client if their scores on a measure were shown to be relatively stable. This can be achieved by the measure being administered several times prior to their attending counselling. This is important as it is known that when administering a measure for a second time, the scores for a subsequent administration tend to regress towards the mean. These shortcomings raise the issue of whether practitioners have to adopt only a quantitative approach. If the aim of the practitioner is to evaluate change, then given that change is a multifaceted phenomenon, then the tools to evaluate it must also be multifaceted and incorporate both nomothetic (standardized) and ideographic (individual) data as well as qualitative and quantitative approaches. Each of these approaches is addressed in this chapter.

Using a core battery

Focusing for the moment on a quantitative approach, a central issue concerns what measures are to be used to evaluate counselling. One strategy is to employ components of a 'core battery'. Such a core battery might comprise three levels: global, specific and personal. The *global* level might be evaluated using the Symptom Checklist-90R (SCL-90R) (Derogatis, 1983) which comprises items addressing nine dimensions (depression, anxiety, hostility, etc.). In addition, the Inventory of Interpersonal Problems (IIP) (Horowitz et al., 1988) presents as a complementary measure tapping a range of interpersonal issues. Both these measures would provide a broad overview of clients' presenting problems with norms available for the SCL-90R and the increasing use of the IIP likely to lead to norms being devised. The *specific* level would comprise a measure deemed particularly suited to the focus of the client's focal issues. However, this level of evaluation may be optional. The third level can be described as *personal*. One example of this level of evaluation is the use of ideographic data derived from instruments in which clients devise the items. For example, the Personal Questionnaire approach (PQ) (Mulhall, 1976) invites clients to identify items which are uniquely meaningful to them: for example, 'Concern about my dementing mother.' This item is unlikely to be part of any standardized measure but for one particular client this item may encapsulate their major worry.

Data from standardized measures (that is, primarily the first and second levels) can be easily presented as group data (that is, the mean pre- and post-counselling scores for a particular cohort of clients). Data can also be presented in a format which shows whether or not individual clients meet certain specific criteria for reliable and clinically significant improvement. These procedures, which only require a pocket calculator, have been summarized elsewhere (see Barkham, 1992).

Quantitative evaluation of the process of outcome

An important issue in evaluation is addressing, or rather redressing, the balance between counselling process and outcome. Counselling outcome probably has primary interest for managers and administrators. However, constituent components of the counselling process are also paramount (for example the client–counsellor relationship). Indeed, a client's capacity to develop a meaningful and working relationship with their counsellor may be a central means of evaluating the overall effectiveness of counselling for a particular client. One way of achieving a rapprochement between process and outcome evaluations is to make evaluation an ongoing process throughout counselling rather than the simplistic pre post application of some outcome measures. There is understandable concern about whether the change reflected by pre post scores can adequately summarize the change process. What is required is an evaluation which is seen to tap the essential components of the counselling process. The use of an ongoing strategy also addresses some practical problems arising when clients fail to return forms at the end of counselling. Accordingly, not only does this strategy protect against drop-outs failing to provide end-of-counselling evaluations but, more importantly, it provides an ongoing account of the client's progress. This can then provide the counsellor with important information when approaching the end of the contract.

Some useful candidates for providing the ongoing evaluation include the PQ method described earlier. In addition to the item being selected by the client, the form can be completed in a few seconds: the number of items ranging from two to ten. Indeed, items could be added during the course of counselling, reflecting the process that the central issues for the client often change as a function of counselling.

Qualitative approaches to process and outcome

One useful way of tapping clients' perceptions of the content of the session is to ask clients to identify what it was that they found most helpful in a counselling session. One way of doing this is to use a variant of Llewelyn et al.'s (1988) Helpful Aspects of Therapy (HAT) questionnaire. This questionnaire asks the client to write down both what they found most helpful and, equally important, most hindering in the preceding session. This strategy is based on what has been termed the 'events paradigm' in which the purpose is to collect data on one particular class of phenomenon in the counselling process (for example, helpful events). Equally, tapping clients' overall impressions of what they have gained at the end of counselling can provide powerful and insightful data with which to counterbalance the more quantitative approaches.

General guidelines

When requiring clients to complete forms of any kind, there can be a tendency to present this as an 'option' or equally to present it in a half-hearted way. What is important is that clients can be presented with a clear and understandable rationale for why they are being asked to complete any forms. Another point concerns the timing of completing forms. It is worth considering the potential downside of clients completing forms immediately after a counselling session due to emotional distress or fatigue. Equally, if the practitioner is asking for their impressions of the session, it may be only after some time that the client experiences the real impact of the session (later in the day or the week). It can often pay dividends to ask clients to complete forms prior to a session, especially if you are interested in the extent to which they have assimilated or worked on issues raised in previous sessions. Also, it can often serve to focus the client on the work in hand.

From evaluation to research

Carrying out some or all of the above procedures may lead some practitioners to ask whether they can set up the evaluation within some more formal design which may then address specific research questions. One step towards adopting a research framework is to view each client as a single case study. This approach would enable each case to act as a replication of the previous case, thereby setting up a clinical replication series in which a body of knowledge about counselling process and outcome was gradually accrued. Another approach might be to decide on a number of ongoing projects within the counselling practice with each client being allocated to the project which is most applicable to them. The issues arising from adopting a practitioner-scientist approach to process and outcome research are addressed elsewhere (Elton Wilson and Barkham, in press) as are the varied research approaches available to the aspiring practitioner-scientist (for example Parry and Watts, 1989).

References

Barkham, M. (1992) 'Understanding, implementing and presenting counselling evaluation', in R. Bayne and P. Nicolson (eds), *Counselling and Psychology for Health Professionals*. London: Chapman & Hall.

Derogatis, L.R. (1983) *The SCL-90R: Administration, Scoring and Procedures – Manual II*. Towson, MD: Clinical Psychometric Research.

Elton Wilson, J. and Barkham, M. (in press) 'A practitioner-scientist approach to psychotherapy process and outcome research', in P. Clarkson and M. Pokorny (eds), *Handbook of Psychotherapy*. London: Routledge.

Horowitz, L.M., Rosenberg, S.E., Baer, B.A., Ureno, G. and Villasenor, V.S. (1988) 'Inventory of Interpersonal Problems: psychometric properties and clinical applications', *Journal of Consulting and Clinical Psychology*, 56: 885–92.

Llewelyn, S.P., Elliott, R., Shapiro, D.A. Hardy, G.E. and Firth-Cozens, J. (1988) 'Client perceptions of significant events in prescriptive and exploratory periods of individual therapy', *British Journal of Clinical Psychology*, 27: 105–14.

Maxwell, R.J. (1984) 'Quality assessment in health', *British Medical Journal*, 288: 1470–2.

Mulhall, D.J. (1976) 'Systematic self-assessment by PQRST', *Psychological Medicine*, 6: 591–7.

Parry, G. (1992) 'Improving psychotherapy services: applications of research, audit and evaluation', *British Journal of Clinical Psychology*, 31: 3–19.

Parry, G. and Watts, F.N. (1989) *Behavioural and Mental Health Research: A Handbook of Skills and Methods*. Hove and London: Erlbaum.

27 Starting your own private practice

I am a trainee counsellor and eventually hope to start in private practice. At what stage in my professional development should I contemplate such a move and how do I go about it?

Gladeana McMahon and Ken Powell

As a trainee counsellor you will need to develop your competency until you can cope with and deal with the great majority of clients who present themselves to you. In private practice you will also need to be able to work by yourself, largely without the outside help and support provided by counselling agencies and organizations.

To reach this point we would suggest the following process as a typical path to be followed. Others might advise you differently but it has worked for us in developing nearly forty years' successful practice between us.

Training

Good counsellors never stop learning. Whether through short courses, seminars, books, magazines or by learning from others, developing relevant skills continues throughout your working life. As a trainee counsellor you need both general and specialist training to provide you with a sound theoretical base.

For general training, we would recommend a generic basic counselling skills course of at least 450 hours duration. Many colleges offer one-, two- or three-year diploma courses. Apart from basic counselling skills, many of these courses offer the opportunity of developing specialist skills together with providing an overview of differing theoretical orientations.

There are many theoretical schools – humanistic, analytical, cognitive, behavioural and transpersonal being the five main approaches. Even when you have selected a particular approach you will still find it helpful to have at least a working knowledge of alternative theoretical models.

It is important that you recognize that no single model can

provide all the answers to all situations (whatever its protagonists might claim!). In the longer term, you may wish to experiment with different therapeutic approaches, trying out techniques on fellow trainees first; fitting the treatment to the client and not the client to the treatment model. The more tools you have at your disposal to use, the more clients you can help.

You should also consider taking specialist training on subjects such as sexual abuse, eating disorders, trauma counselling, sexuality, etc. Additionally, an understanding of psychiatric disorders such as depression, psychosis and PTSD (Post-Traumatic Stress Disorder) is invaluable in helping you assess the needs of your client and whether you are the most appropriate person to meet these. Although specialist training is essential you also need to be aware of the negative aspects of labelling clients.

Personal therapy

Professional opinion is divided as to whether personal therapy is necessary for professional development and, if so, over what period and at what frequency. In extreme schools of thought, personal therapy of three to five times a week over a five-year period is deemed necessary. The other extreme says that no personal therapy is ever needed.

We take the view that you will not be able to identify with the risks a client takes unless you have been a client yourself in individual counselling. We feel that personal therapy once a week for a year would be invaluable.

Personal therapy can help in other ways:

1 by examining your own particular hang ups, blocks, motivations and prejudices (and we all have them!) you will be able to recognize their emergence in your interactions with clients;
2 by observing how your therapist helps you deal with your own personal 'gremlins' you will pick up useful techniques yourself.

Ideally you need to undergo personal therapy as soon as possible after embarking on your initial training.

Professional supervision

Of equal importance with training and personal therapy, professional supervision is what will help you work effectively with clients. A professional supervisor will look objectively at how you handle your clients (especially the more problematic ones) and through the process of supervision help you improve your therapeutic skills.

The supervisor can also be used as a safety valve or support in difficult situations and be able to guide you regarding professional ethics. Some may even be able to provide you with good business advice.

Experience

Experience or practice makes perfect (or nearly perfect). To start with, your counselling with clients needs to be in a protected or supported environment where help is close at hand. You will be understandably nervous at seeing your first clients whilst trying to make theory and practice come together for you. You will probably fall into the traps of categorizing or labelling clients or their behaviour, of trying to impose your solutions on them, of not listening properly, of being afraid to challenge them when it would be helpful, of not being sure of when to refer on, etc., etc. There are countless mistakes to be made and you will make them, as we have.

Ideally you will have been working with clients during your training and will have had the opportunity of taking what you have learnt back to your organization to be put into practice. As your ability grows, you need to seek experience with as wide a range of clients and client problems as youth counselling, for example, won't help you understand the needs of a middle-aged bereaved person.

If you intend to offer a limited range of counselling services to a specific client group, you may find that two or three years experience is sufficient. However, if you intend to be able to cope with most clients and client problems then you are likely to need at least five years practice to experience a full range of problems and acquire the confidence to deal with them. Clearly one option is to start with your own particular interest or specialism but with further training to enlarge what you offer as your abilities develop.

Understanding professional ethics and legal liabilities

If you are to run a private practice you need to have an understanding of the law and its implications for you and your practice, for example, confidentiality and under what circumstances you can be forced to break this.

You need to consider the issues of professional liability and cover together with the advisability of belonging to a professional association with a recognized code of ethics and practice and a complaints procedure such as that used by the British Association for Counselling.

How would you handle the 9 p.m. client who is suicidal or the psychotic who needs sectioning? Issues of personal safety and how to keep your client notes secure have to be considered. If you are working from home you will need to check your insurance policies and whether your local authority allows you to run a business from your home.

Personal assessment and motivation

Becoming self-employed is a big step, in addition to your professional competence, you need to assess your own motivation, your ability to develop and to drive your own business, your self-reliance and self-discipline.

Starting a private practice

If you are seriously contemplating private practice in the near future we would recommend the booklet *Starting Your Own Private Practice: A Basic Guide to Self-Employment* (Powell and McMahon, 1993) as essential reading. It covers all the areas to which you need to give attention. Here we can only give you a flavour of what is involved in two or three of the many aspects concerned with running your own business.

Research and planning

The worst thing you can do is to wander into private practice without adequate research and planning. Fundamentally, you need to generate sufficient income to cover your business expenses and provide you with an acceptable standard of living. How can this be done?

The key, not surprisingly, is the client. As the well-known management guru Peter Drucker would say 'Creating a client or customer is the main objective of any business', so the first research you need to undertake is to answer the following questions:

Who are my potential clients?
Where are they likely to live?
How far would they be prepared to travel?
What level of fees are they likely to be prepared to pay?
How do I make them aware of the services I offer?

The sort of answers you are likely to come up with will vary according to where you live or practise and the services you offer. If you practise in a deprived working-class area your answers will be very different from those with a Harley Street practice.

Typically, you may find that most of your potential clients are likely to be in professional jobs (or whose partners are), and are likely to live within about a 3-mile radius of your practice, can frequently only make evening appointments, are prepared to pay an hourly fee in the range of £15–£30 and are likely to come upon your name in the Yellow Pages or some other directory or reference source.

Financial planning

How much income might you expect to generate from fee-paying clients? Will it be enough for you to live on?

You may decide, for example, that you would be happy with twenty clients per week each paying £20 for a weekly 60-minute session over a working year of forty weeks, giving a total income of £16,000. If, at the same time, you reckon that it may take you twelve months to build your caseload up to this level, then your first year's income will be more like £8000. After allowing for business expenses (advertising, stationery, travel, equipment, heating, lighting, etc.) and tax you may find yourself left with only £5000 to live on in your first year.

We cannot emphasize enough how important it is to do this sort of calculation before you throw up your job and set up on your own. Ideally, you should draw up a month-by-month cash forecast, not forgetting any initial capital you may need to equip your consulting room or spend on advertising.

When you have done your sums, covering at least your first year of private practice, you will probably find that one of the following options is necessary for you to survive:

1 If you have any savings you may need to draw heavily on these to finance yourself in the early months (a figure of £5000 may not be unrealistic).
2 You may have an obliging partner who is prepared to finance you or share some of the costs.
3 You may need to see and persuade your bank manager to give you a loan.
4 You may decide to keep your present job and run your private practice in the evenings and weekends (if you have the stamina) or, alternatively, reduce your present job to part-time, possibly with a job-share arrangement.

Whichever of these applies will depend largely on your personal circumstances. Remember, the *only* reason businesses fail is because they run out of cash. It sounds simple to avoid but thousands of small businesses fail because of under-capitalization, being over-optimistic or just not doing their sums at all!

Other considerations

1 When you have done all these things then, hopefully, you have got the makings of a credible business plan. But you are not finished yet. At the end of your financial year the taxman will be chasing you for your accounts and if they are not ready and audited he is likely to assess you at a higher level than necessary. You will also need to have put money aside to pay your tax.

2 You may, if you are not familiar with book-keeping practice, need to obtain the advice of an accountant and you will need one anyway to audit your books and present your accounts to the tax man.

3 Decide how you will collect income from your clients. Will they pay after each session or will you invoice them monthly?

4 Set up a separate business bank account otherwise your private expenditure will get mixed up with your business expenditure and become very difficult to untangle.

5 When you have been running your business for, perhaps, six months, take the time to review how well (or how badly) things are going. Are you getting sufficient clients? Are you spending more than you thought? What do you need to do to get back on schedule or improve the business further?

Good businesses monitor themselves all the time and never become complacent. Opportunities and threats are spotted promptly and plans are changed accordingly. You'll need to do the same.

Reference

Powell, K. and McMahon, G. (1993) *Starting Your Own Private Practice: A Basic Guide to Self-Employment*. Loughton, Essex: Gale Centre Publications.

28   Objections to private practice

I understand that you are an opponent of private practice in counselling. What are your objections?

David Pilgrim

What is wrong with private practice in counselling?

I would like to address private practice under two sub-headings, which reflect general and particular ways of looking at the above question. First, there is a difference between justifying private practice on pragmatic grounds and justifying it on ethical grounds. Second, there are some particular considerations that apply to counselling and psychotherapy which need to be taken into account when discussing private practice.

Pragmatics and ethics

There are a variety of pragmatic justifications for being involved in private practice as a client. Indeed, I was a private client myself because in seeking therapy as a trainee in the NHS, publicly provided therapy was not available in my locality. Not surprisingly I have the most sympathy (not just empathy) for *clients* who have few or no options. Likewise whilst I refuse to join a private medical insurance scheme, if my child had a life threatening or painful medical condition I might pay for their treatment if the NHS could not deliver it quickly. I would do so under pressure and with the guilty awareness that a poorer neighbour with the same plight might not be able to jump the queue in the same way. So the client predicament about private practice immediately reveals a central consideration about why private practice is ethically untenable – it must favour those who can afford to pay and penalize those who cannot. It is ipso facto discriminatory. Whilst this claim could be made for *all* services from restaurants to car hire, there is a particular ethical problem for me about people who are already physically or emotionally distressed either being impoverished by payment or being excluded from the service because the fees cannot be met. On these grounds alone private practice is simply unethical.

There are pragmatic justifications for practising privately as a practitioner. Having escaped the vagaries of NHS clinical work (though to the less financially rewarding life of being an academic) I realize that it is easy for me to be purist about the evils of working privately. Friends and clinician colleagues of mine who, in younger days, eschewed private practice (and who still espouse left of centre social values), are now working partly outside the public sector. I can see this leading to full-time private practice in a short time. Their work context over the past ten years has been restructured and destabilized by a ruthless government regime which has sought to privatize public services or make them run by the rules of the market. None of us are immune from pressure of this type. The whole socially regressive regime since 1979 has pushed ordinary decent people into individualism and away from collective responsibility. It has appealed to anti-social impulses of selfishness and greed, whether it has been about buying BUPA membership or shares for commodities that the public were already supposed to own.

In these circumstances, the wider political context has both legitimized the notion that the cash nexus is honourable, rather than corrupting and discriminatory, and it has degraded the quality of life of health and welfare employees. Not surprisingly private practice has become an escape route for disaffected practitioners. For me, this still does not make private practice ethical but it does make it understandable. Like all workers, they have a right to seek more acceptable conditions of work. Moreover, sometimes laudable experiments can only take place by working outside of the public sector, because of its dominance by groups like the medical profession which are notorious for their conservatism and lack of imagination about healing practices. In the field of mental health the therapeutic houses of Arbours and the Philadelphia Association could not have been constructed inside the NHS because of the one-dimensional views that psychiatrists have about the treatment of 'schizophrenia'.

Leaving aside these innovations made possible by working outside traditional state organizations, I still sense an underlying sense of guilt from many practitioners who switch to private work, revealed by the euphemisms that have been invented to disguise the contract. We hear of people working 'independently' or 'going freelance'. Why is the spade of private practice not always called a spade? What does that tell us about its dubious ethical status?

Now that I have rehearsed these general arguments about pragmatics and ethics let me turn to the specifics of counselling and psychotherapy.

Particular considerations about private counselling and therapy

First, there is the argument that in counselling (not other forms of healing practice) paying a fee is a positive contribution to the client's welfare – ensuring their motivation and symbolizing that the contract is taken seriously. A second, related argument from those with a psychodynamic bent is that the fee becomes a crucial focus for communications about love and hate of the therapist. The argument then runs that the absence of the fee would actually *deprive* the client of a vital arena for learning about themselves. Both of these arguments have a superficial cogency. However, the views of the dead patriarch Freud are ambiguous on these points. Sometimes he considered the fee to be an indispensable part of psychoanalysis (Freud, 1913/1968: 132) and yet he envisaged a future with free therapy (Freud, 1918/1968: 167). Also, during its early days, before fee-paying became ubiquitous and obligatory, the German Psychoanalytic Society in Berlin and Vienna required its members to treat one patient free (Eissler, 1974).

In addition to these ambiguities from the psychoanalytical old guard there is the simple empirical point – where is the evidence that paying for your personal learning leads to a superior outcome? I know of no evidence in the vastly researched area of psychotherapy process and outcome that demonstrates such a relationship unambiguously. Again, the sparseness of the literature on the particular topic of the fee might suggest an associated guilt. Researchers and their respondents (therapists) might consider it a rather unsavoury topic for examination (see Power and Pilgrim, 1990, for a summary of the research in this area).

Of course there is a more cynical interpretation of why the fee is given such centrality as a *therapeutic* not contractual issue – it legitimizes the right of private practitioners to take money off people and feel positive about it. For me, trying to make a virtue of a vice in this way does not ennoble practitioners. To draw a comparison with prostitution, sex workers are traditional icons of immorality and yet they are not as hypocritical as private therapists and counsellors. The former make no claims that the fee is there in the interests of the client. Nor do sex workers primarily seek their own sexual gratification, which cannot always be said to be the case for private counsellors and psychotherapists. In a recent study, 65 per cent of practitioners claimed that they had encountered clients who had had a prior sexual involvement with another therapist (cited in Fasal and Edwards, 1992).

Private practice is particularly vulnerable to a lack of regulation and monitoring. In the public sector there are monitoring mechanisms within the professions to ensure good practice. Even if private practitioners become registered in the future, their isolated work context provides a more vulnerable setting for abuse of clients to take place. In one of the first surveys of sexual contact with clients, Forer in 1968 reported that 17 per cent of male psychologists in private practice in Los Angeles confirmed such contact, whereas none was reported in therapists working in institutional settings (unpublished paper cited in Pope et al., 1986).

With regard to the pressures to work privately because of the absence of opportunities in the public sector, counselling and psychotherapy are *not* like some forms of alternative healing practices. In the case, for instance, of osteopathy, there are particular historical reasons, to do with medical exclusion, that have kept the practice (to date) outside of the NHS. Counselling and psychotherapy are legitimate practices in salaried educational, voluntary sector, mental health and primary care services. Thus there is no organizational or legal reason why people *have* to work privately.

My final specific doubt about private practice is that clients are being asked to pay for a 'product' which is of dubious efficacy. Whilst I am not against therapy or counselling in principle (cf. Masson, 1989), as I have argued elsewhere, the best that can be said about talking treatments is that they are of marginal utility (Pilgrim, 1992). This being the case, I would warn any prospective client to be aware that involvement with a therapist or counsellor might lead in their case to substantial personal help, or it might be a waste of time and money, or they might feel worse after the contact than before. The overall figures on outcome suggest any of these three scenarios are possible for individual clients. If the latter two prevail *and* the client has paid for the 'privilege' of either not being helped or deteriorating, then this seems to raise particular ethical considerations which therapists and counsellors need to take seriously.

References

Eissler, K.R. (1974) 'On some theoretical and technical problems regarding the payment of fees for psychoanalytical treatment', *International Review of Psychoanalysis*, 1: 713–21.

Fasal, J. and Edwards, M. (1992) 'Keeping an intimate relationship professional', *Openmind*, 57: 10–11.

Freud, S. (1913/1968) 'On beginning the treatment', pp. 123–44 in J. Strachey (ed.), *Complete Works of Sigmund Freud*, Vol. 12. London: Hogarth Press.

Freud, S. (1918/1968) 'Lines of advance in psychoanalytic therapy', pp. 159–68 in J. Strachey (ed.), *Complete Works of Sigmund Freud*, Vol. 17. London: Hogarth Press.

Masson, J. (1989) *Against Therapy*. London: Harper Collins.

Pilgrim, D. (1992) 'Psychotherapy and political evasions', in W. Dryden and C. Feltham (eds), *Psychotherapy and Its Discontents*. Buckingham: Open University Press.

Pope, K.S., Keith-Speigel, P. and Tabachnick, B.G. (1986) 'Sexual attraction to clients', *American Psychologist*, 41(2): 147–58.

Power, L. and Pilgrim, D. (1990) 'The fee in psychotherapy: practitioners' accounts', *Counselling Psychology Quarterly*, 3(2): 153–7.

29 Against indemnity insurance

*Our counselling tutors insist that we take out
indemnity insurance. I hear that you refuse to be
so insured. Why is this?*

Dave Mearns

It has become fashionable within the profession of counselling to
take out indemnity insurance. This insurance is not at all expensive
with a £1,000,000 worth of cover being available for a mere £37,
a premium which shows an 8 per cent reduction on the equivalent
rate six years ago. Perhaps this reduction in premium is not
surprising since, according to the two main brokerage firms, *there
has never been a significant claim in Great Britain in connection
with a counselling subscriber.*

Indemnity insurance provides cover for civil action against the
practitioner on the grounds of professional *malpractice, errors* or
omissions. However, this is not to say that every *error* we make as
practitioners is punishable by civil judgment. Both English and
Scottish law require that the test of *reasonable behaviour* be met.
In essence, we are not required to display best possible practice,
but simply to undertake to bring a fair, reasonable and competent
degree of skill to our work. Civil claims for error in counselling
would be more difficult to pursue than in the medical world where
the practitioner's work may be physically intrusive and where it is
easier to relate damage to treatment. A civil action could proceed
on the ground of *omission* if, for example, we negligently missed
an appointment thus causing our client financial loss in some way.
However, although this would technically constitute a case, it is
difficult to imagine it ever being pursued. Certainly, instances of
physical or sexual abuse by the counsellor could rightly result in
civil action for *malpractice* and emotional abuse might be the basis
for a case, albeit even more difficult to pursue.

Indemnity insurance should not be confused with other forms of
insurance which have a different relevance for the counsellor. For
example, *public liability* covers the counsellor against physical
injury incurred by clients visiting his or her premises and for
damage to third parties caused by those premises (for example,
damage caused to neighbouring buildings by a fire starting in the

counsellor's office). *Employer's liability* may also be relevant in counselling practices which hire support staff or where the practice is run by senior partners employing other counsellors. *Home insurance* and *car insurance* might be declared void if the home or car was used in connection with the counselling business, even if a claim had nothing to do with the counselling work (usually these are covered at little or no cost by simply informing the insurance companies). Modern policies also usually include an element for *product liability*. This offers cover against the physical products of the business causing injury or damage to another person or property. It is difficult to conceive the relevance of this to counselling unless, for example, the relaxation tape which we sell creates overheating in the purchaser's tape recorder!

I heartily support the purchase of public liability and employer's liability insurance as well as taking the advice on informing home and car insurers. Also, I provide information and forms relating to indemnity insurance for students on my courses and support their purchase of this insurance if that gives them peace of mind or if it is a requirement of the counselling agency in which they are working (for example health centres occasionally look for such insurance because that is customary in the medical sector). However, personally, I regard the whole notion of indemnity insurance within counselling with considerable derision. Perhaps it confers some obscure status on the individual who can boast as I have overheard: 'a £1,000,000 worth of cover'. I fear that the attraction of indemnity insurance may reflect some underlying lack of confidence within the profession which likens itself in some way to the medical domain in its perceived need for insurance against civil claims. In fact, this need for insurance in a profession which is neither physically intrusive nor creates concrete products is largely illusory as evidenced by the fact that through the many years of existence of indemnity insurance there have been no claims.

However, the existence of indemnity insurance within counselling is not simply a matter for derision but one which could have serious implications. It is a well known fact within insurance circles that *the existence of insurance encourages claims*. This is one reason for the huge number of claims made against medical practitioners in the USA where, on average, *every* gynaecologist will settle a claim for 'malpractice' 1.25 times in his or her career. This fact that legal claims are fostered by the existence of insurance is recognized in the 'Advice to members' given by one insurance scheme: 'Do not inform clients that you are covered by insurance as this may increase the risk of you being sued.' In a profession which prizes open and honest relating between counsellor and client I find such advice to be distasteful, but not as flagrantly immoral as the requirement of insurers that the counsellor must deny liability if challenged by the client regardless of any responsibility the counsellor might feel. At best this dishonesty is likely to alienate the client and at worst it would create mystification and the compounding of any abuse the client may have experienced.

Another difficulty I have with indemnity insurance in relation to counselling concerns the implications it may have concerning the nature of *responsibility* within the client–counsellor relationship. Indemnity insurance comes from other professional realms such as law and medicine where the practitioner is accepted as being an *expert* on the client's or patient's problem. The practitioner in these professions is not acting as a facilitator, but as an advisor and director of the action or treatment. Hence the service offered in these other realms is expert-centred rather than client-centred as that phrase is espoused in the *Code of Ethics and Practice* of the British Association for Counselling (BAC, 1991). The definition of *reasonable behaviour* is not easy to construct within an expert-centred profession, but it is an absolute minefield in a client-centred, facilitating role. For example, would the counsellor be *negligent*, that is to say would he or she have behaved 'unreasonably' in none, one or both of the following scenarios?

1 The client talks about the possibility of his suicide. The counsellor does not speak directly against that possibility. The next week the client commits suicide.
2 The client talks about the possibility of his suicide. The counsellor argues vigorously against this. The counsellor's bias encourages a counter-reaction in the client who argues more vehemently in favour of suicide. The next week the client commits suicide.

Although sectors of the counselling profession are sufficiently sophisticated in their understanding of human dynamics to know the dangers of encouraging reaction in clients, the counsellor in the second scenario is less likely to be regarded as negligent because he or she *appeared* to take action against suicide. Indemnity insurance reinforces this position by providing cover against any neglect, error or omission in providing treatment or advice in the course of the work.

Perhaps it might even be argued that taking insurance against this risk is a de facto admission that this is a basis for a claim. In the area of *errors* it would be very difficult to define the legal role of the counsellor. The danger is that counsellors, by aligning with the medical profession over the issue of insurance, may similarly become viewed as responsible *for* the client rather than responsible *to* the client. This difference is crucial to a role where the practitioner seeks to empower rather than take responsibility away from the client. The issue of responsibility needs to be teased out and debated within counselling circles. Hopefully that debate will take place before major counselling agencies or associations begin to demand indemnity insurance for their members.

As counselling develops, the danger of its institutionalization increases. Many of the checks and balances which are put in place, like guidelines on standards and ethics, accreditation criteria and anti-discriminatory policies are very important in the overall balance they create. But it is possible to go too far in prescriptions for the nature of responsibility within counselling. If we adopt medical conventions like requiring indemnity insurance then we risk making a fundamental alteration to the nature of responsibility in the counselling relationship with the practitioner being regarded not as a facilitator of the client's growth, but as a director of that growth.

My personal stance against indemnity insurance seeks to encourage debate of the issues involved. Thus far, insurance schemes have become recommended within counselling circles without this examination of the present and future implications. Indeed, such is the naivety on indemnity insurance that I have often heard it argued that such insurance is important for the *protection of the client* and that the counsellor is actually being responsible to his client by taking insurance. Nothing could be further from the truth: indemnity insurance is a combatant defensive action taken to discourage possible challenge from clients.

Reference

BAC (1991) *Code of Ethics and Practice for Counsellors*. Rugby: British Association for Counselling.

30 Making a living as a counsellor

What are the difficulties in making a living as a counsellor?

Colin Feltham

I have found the difficulties in earning sufficient money from counselling real, enduring, numerous and rarely openly discussed. Intending trainees and those currently training deserve honest information on the problems confronting them when considering a career in counselling. Among those who make the best living from counselling are probably the proprietors of training institutes and trainers; arguably, it is not in their interests to welcome candid discussion of a negative subject like this if they wish to encourage a steady stream of paying trainees. The list of difficulties given below is pertinent to practice in the UK only and is based on the assumption that such difficulties are likely to be experienced by *most* practitioners, rather than only by a few who may be untalented or faint-hearted. I hope these points may stimulate a debate that is long overdue.

Baseline considerations

Most counsellors are attracted to the work for other than financial reasons. You may be in the fortunate position of not *needing* to work for the money (for example, if you have an affluent enough partner; if you are retired; or if you earn sufficient money from one job and intend counselling to be simply an interesting sideline). If you are not in such a position, do realistically consider the level of income you need to support your present lifestyle. Like many 'people professions', counselling is not a highly remunerative activity for most practitioners.

The counsellor's expenditure

At first glance the costs involved in becoming and practising as a counsellor may not appear very high. You are likely, however, to incur most of the following costs:

Training
If paying for your own training, the costs are considerable both in time and money. With the demand created by accreditation, courses have become longer and more expensive. Arguably, the better (or more prestigious) courses are more expensive. Some potentially excellent counsellors (I have met some of them) cannot get beyond this first financial hurdle and are forced to surrender their aspirations. Since counsellors are expected to engage in on-going professional development, you must reckon to spend still more on training after qualifying. (I recall a woman publicly complaining about the cost of a counselling conference that I had helped to organize; she was, I believe, a single parent on a very low income and clearly a minority delegate among a majority of more comfortably off delegates.)

Supervision
Many training courses require you to pay for your own supervision in addition to course fees. All practising counsellors are obliged to receive *ongoing* supervision. The costs can be substantial.

Personal therapy
Almost all training courses now require you to be in personal therapy or counselling yourself. Some counselling pundits believe that all counsellors should be in *ongoing* therapy. Again, expect high costs.

Professional memberships, accreditation and insurance
You can't practise credibly unless you are a member of a counselling or psychotherapy organization, whose annual subscription you must pay. It is also wise to remain closely affiliated with such organizations because so many referrals come by way of personal recommendations, as do offers of sessional work. (Another way of putting this is that it is important *who you know*.) Credibility as a practitioner increasingly depends on your qualifying status and in order to become and remain accredited you have to pay application fees. You are also likely to need professional insurance, another annual cost.

Equipment
At the time of training, if not thereafter, you may need a tape-recorder and supply of tapes. If you are in private practice, a telephone and answering machine are indispensable. You need some kind of professional stationery and possibly publicity material. If you are not fortunate enough to have a suitable spare

room in your house, you may have to hire a room for your counselling. The cost of books and professional journals is not inconsiderable. You may be able to manage your own accounts, but if not you must pay for book-keeping services. For some, all of the above costs seem minimal; for others, they can be almost insurmountable.

Establishing and promoting a practice

You may well be a good counsellor but a poor entrepreneur. It is well recognized in the commercial world that an excellent product can flop if it is poorly promoted. Clients do not come your way by chance. Many counsellors promote themselves indirectly by writing articles and books, running workshops, networking, etc. Doing a good job with clients and hoping that they will recommend you is only a small *part* of building a reputation. It is worth adding that, since it can take some years to establish yourself, it is preferable that you remain living in the same house or area.

The counsellor's environment and circumstances

The area in which you live partly dictates attitudes to counselling and how much people can pay. I live and work in a part of east London where the 'going rate' for counselling is lower than in northwest London, for example. Although I have no proof, I suspect that clients are generally more impressed by and have greater confidence in counsellors who live and work in smarter areas and in well-appointed houses. Perhaps the fact that some counsellors rent consulting rooms in just such places supports this belief. The layout of your house is also a consideration. Ideally, you will have a suitable room close to an outer door and you will not have young children who shout and scream, leave toys everywhere, and make demands at the very times (usually early evening) when most clients prefer their appointments. If you are a family's main breadwinner, you are well-advised not to attempt to make a living from counselling!

Scattered commitments

I, and most other counsellors I know, cannot rely on income purely from counselling private clients. I have been involved in supervision, training, group facilitation, consultancy, conference organizing and other 'counselling-related' work. I have often had to go where the money is and to spend a lot of time travelling across London for a weekly two hours, here and there, of modestly paid work. The fact that so much counselling work is of a part-time or sessional nature means that you may be very stretched in terms of juggling travelling time and diversity of activities. In spite of the stimulation involved and additions to your CV, you can also run into many professional blind alleys.

Competition for work

Although counsellors do not much talk about competition (indeed many claim rather naively that 'There's such a great need for counsellors'), there are only so many clients to go around. Competition is not direct, but subtle. Psychotherapists put it about that their work is more 'in depth'; the accredited discreetly brandish their accreditation; innovative practitioners attempt to oust traditionalists (and vice versa); newly qualified counsellors offer lower rates; and a great deal of counselling is still provided by volunteers. Totton (1992) tells of an experienced therapist's falling referral rate after a group of therapists began a local training course and competitively trumpeted their exaggerated professional affiliations.

Moral and intellectual qualms

Some counsellors feel strongly that clients in need should be offered counselling even if they can't pay the going rate. Sliding scales, fee bands and free places are ways of addressing this humanitarian concern. To survive as a private practitioner, however, you must strictly limit your humanitarian concerns! You may sometimes realize that a client would be better referred to a colleague or an alternative facility. From time to time, for example, I have felt compelled to advise a potential client that he or she is eligible for free and/or more specialized counselling elsewhere. Another ethical dilemma may occur when the client or counsellor feels that there is no further pressing need for counselling. It is always possible to *find* further interesting material to work on and it is possible and profitable to persuade the client to do so, but I doubt whether it is ethical. Pilgrim (1992) gives an account of political considerations that may disturb (socially aware) counsellors.

Brief counselling

Budman and Gurman (1988) argue that many therapists 'uncon-sciously recognise the fiscal convenience of maintaining long-term clients'. Effective counselling which respects the client's right to decide on which goals to address (and which not to) is often brief. This can mean a high turnover of clients, gaps in one's schedule and an unpredictable income. A colleague tells me that the couple counselling she does is economically less reliable than individual counselling because it is frequently much briefer. Counsellors are not in the economically fortunate position of the psychoanalyst who may see relatively few clients in his or her career, but sees each of them several times a week for several years. Schacter (1992) calculates that 'a full-time analyst will have analysed [only] between 50 and 100 patients in his/her lifetime'.

Scarcity of jobs

Having studiously scanned the job advertisements in the *Guardian* for well over ten years, I can authoritatively say that there are very few counselling jobs. There are certainly more part-time than full-time jobs, but still relatively few. A survey of 559 BAC members by O'Sullivan (1989) revealed that 53 per cent of those describing themselves as counsellors were in paid employment, but only 27 per cent were full time. Of the few full-time jobs advertised, many are highly exclusive. You may be a well qualified and experienced counsellor, but if you happen not to have a psychodynamic orientation, a psychology degree or 'experience in higher education', for example, you may not get a look-in. With newly qualified counsellors flooding on to the job market year by year, you can find that you are in competition with very experienced counsellors who are simply trying to move sideways in an overcrowded profession. Once, when involved in some short-listing, I was staggered to see how overqualified many applicants were for a rather humble counselling position.

The subject is taboo

Yalom (1989), an existentialist group therapist, says that 'in thousands of group meetings, whose members supposedly bare all, I have yet to hear group members disclose their incomes'. Hillman (1982) cites a survey of therapists' attitudes to disclosures about money, and concludes that 'money constellated the ultimate taboo'. Counsellors, like people in general, do not discuss their incomes. Perhaps we are afraid that disclosures about not earning very much may suggest that we are just not very good counsellors. Although I know a few counsellors who appear to do quite well, I have known excellent counsellors who have had to give up counselling to become full-time trainers and social workers instead, because they needed the better or more reliable income. I have never heard this subject openly discussed at counselling conferences.

In conclusion, I believe that you are more likely to 'make it' in counselling if you don't have a dire need to make money, or if you are very single-minded and/or extremely 'cheeky' in marketing yourself. (It may also be significant that a majority of counsellors are women working part-time.) I am hopeful that this depressing situation will change in the years to come, but I advise starry-eyed trainees not to bank on it!

References

Budman, S. and Gurman, A.S. (1988) *Theory and Practice of Brief Therapy*. New York: Guilford.

Hillman, J. (1982) 'A contribution to soul and money', in R.A. Lockhart et al., *Soul and Money*. Dallas: Spring.

O'Sullivan, K. (1989) 'Membership survey of BAC', *Counselling*, 68: 9–15.

Pilgrim, D. (1992) 'Psychotherapy and political evasions', in W. Dryden and C. Feltham (eds), *Psychotherapy and its Discontents*. Buckingham: Open University Press.

Schacter, J. (1992) 'Concepts of termination and post-termination patient–analyst contact', *International Journal of Psycho-analysis*, 73(1): 137–54.

Totton, N. (1992) 'Therapists on the couch', *I-to-I Magazine*, 11: 26–7.

Yalom, I. (1989) *Love's Executioner*. Harmondsworth: Penguin.

About the editor

Windy Dryden is Professor of Counselling at Goldsmiths' College, University of London. He has authored or edited over sixty books including *Rational-Emotive Counselling in Action* (Sage Publications, 1990) and *Daring to be Myself: A Case of Rational-Emotive Therapy*, written with Joseph Yankura (Open University Press, 1992). In addition, he edits nine book series in the area of counselling and psychotherapy including the *Whurr Psychotherapy Series* (Whurr Publishers) and *Improve Your Counselling* (Sage Publications). His major interests are in rational-emotive therapy, eclecticism and integration in psychotherapy and, increasingly, writing short, accessible self-help books for the general public.

About the contributors

Waseem J. Alladin is Consultant Clinical Psychologist and Co-Director of the Centre for Mood Disorders, Parklands Mental Health Services, and is based in the Psychology Department, West Park Hospital, Epsom, Surrey

Mark Aveline is a Consultant Psychotherapist in Nottingham

Michael Barkham is a Research Clinical Psychologist working at the MRC/ESRC Social and Applied Psychology Unit, University of Sheffield

Tim Bond is Staff Tutor in Counselling, Department of Adult and Continuing Education, University of Durham

Michael Carroll is Director of Studies in Psychology and Counselling, Roehampton Institute, London

Jocelyn Chaplin is a Feminist Counsellor in independent practice, West London

Emmy van Deurzen-Smith is Dean of the School of Psychotherapy and Counselling, Regent's College, London

Jenifer Elton Wilson is Head of the Counselling and Psychological Services of the University of the West of England, Bristol

Colin Feltham is Course Director, Diploma in Counselling, Thameslink Healthcare Services, Dartford, Kent

Francesca Inskipp is a Freelance Counsellor, Supervisor and Trainer, St Leonards-on-Sea, East Sussex

Michael Jacobs is Director of the Counselling and Psychotherapy Certificate Programme, Department of Adult Education, University of Leicester

Elke Lambers is Co-Director of PCT (Person Centred Therapy) Britain

Gladeana McMahon is a Freelance Counsellor, Supervisor and Trainer in Blackheath, London

Dave Mearns is Director of the Counselling Unit in the Faculty of Education, Strathclyde University, Glasgow

John C. Norcross is Professor and Chair of Psychology, University of Scranton, Scranton, Pennsylvania, USA

Vanja Orlans is a Chartered Psychologist and has a private practice in Counselling and Gestalt Psychotherapy in London

David Pilgrim is Lecturer in Health and Social Welfare at the Open University, Milton Keynes

Ken Powell was, until his death, a Chartered Psychologist in independent practice in London and Cheltenham

Peter Ross is University Counsellor at University of Reading

John Rowan is an independent Psychotherapist who lives and works in Walthamstow, London

Julia Segal is a Counsellor at the CMH Multiple Sclerosis Unit, Central Middlesex Hospital Trust, London

Brian Thorne is Director of Student Counselling and of the Centre for Counselling Studies, University of East Anglia, Norwich

Thomas J. Tomcho is Research Assistant in Psychology, University of Scranton, Scranton, Pennsylvania, USA

Moira Walker is Head of the Counselling Service at Leicester University

Sue Wheeler is Lecturer in Counselling in the School of Continuing Studies, University of Birmingham

Index